the author

David Duncombe is the chaplain for the
School of Medicine at Yale University and
was formerly a lecturer in the Yale Divinity School. As chaplain and religious instructor at a boys' preparatory school he
became interested in assessing the growth
of faith under his guidance. It is that interest which has grown into this book.

Dr. Duncombe has a B.A. degree in gov-
ernment from Dartmouth College, an
M.A. in Christian ethics and law from
Union Theological Seminary, a B.D. in the
psychology of religion and a Ph.D. in religion in higher education and psychology of
religion from Yale University.

the
SHAPE
of the
CHRISTIAN LIFE

the

SHAPE
of the
CHRISTIAN LIFE

DAVID C. DUNCOMBE

nashville ABINGDON PRESS *new york*

THE SHAPE OF THE CHRISTIAN LIFE

Standard Book Number: 687-38339-0

Library of Congress Catalog Card Number: 70-84718

SET UP, PRINTED AND BOUND BY THE
PARTHENON PRESS, AT NASHVILLE,
TENNESSEE, UNITED STATES OF AMERICA

ACKNOWLEDGMENTS

The help given me in writing this book is significant. The study on which it is based culminated in a doctoral dissertation that presents the substance of the book in more detail. It was my work with James E. Dittes at Yale that opened the way to both the clinical and the experimental approaches to the problem of describing the mature Christian life. He also encouraged me to revise my dissertation into book form and provided valuable criticism of the early drafts. Hans W. Frei was my theological conscience, at times suffering as do most consciences when their voices go unheeded. Randolph Crump Miller saw the study develop stage by stage and gave generously of his time and critical abilities.

Also lending valuable assistance were David Little, Jane Mc-Farland, and Raymond P. Morris, who were helpful in suggesting techniques of combining a theological and an empirical study; Clarence L. Bruninga, who sharpened my clinical awareness and also read the early drafts of this book; and Kenneth Underwood, who as director of the Danforth Study of Campus Ministries made possible the first program of evaluation in Christian maturity based upon the method described in this book. Special thanks is also due Yale University and its many ways of keeping a student financially afloat during the years when our family expanded from two to five.

Of the many persons whose encouragement and support aided in ways less easy to enumerate, my wife Sally has contributed the most to the substance of the study. To her the book is dedicated in token of her dedication to me and to the concern expressed in these pages.

Spring, 1968
New Haven, Connecticut

CONTENTS

INTRODUCTION

The Christian Question . . .

"Why should I go to church?" A deceptively simple question, it is whined sooner or later by nearly every child at Sunday breakfast and perhaps echoed silently by their parents during the trials of preparing for the weekly pilgrimage. The question is raised in the pulpit, at the dormitory bull session, on the street corner, and from the depths of solitude. The tone may be pensive, rebellious, despairing, or flippant. Form and circumstance can differ at each asking, but the question remains the same. It is perhaps the crucial Christian question of our day.

. . . Gets a Dishonest Answer . . .

Consider for a moment the common answer, "Going to church is good for you." Many an admonition has been given (and sermon preached) on this theme without awareness of the fundamental dishonesty involved. The dishonesty is not basically in what is said or how it is argued but in the presumption that anything can be said.

Who knows whether a person is *better* for having gone to church?

... If We Take It on Faith

To *know* that the institutional church makes a person a better—or worse—Christian is not a matter of simply stating it, wishing it, or believing it. Nor is it something that a faithful Christian can take on faith. Rather, it requires that we reflect on the nature of *verifiable knowledge* as such knowledge seeks to define and concretely identify the shape of the Christian life. Hopefully, the following chapters may aid in this reflection. But if nothing more, they may indicate the crucial importance of this task for the survival and growth of Christianity.

One Minister's Dilemma

This book grows out of a *professional* concern for the church, especially with the minister's responsibility for enabling growth in the Christian life. I began my own ministry as a chaplain and instructor in religion at a boys' preparatory school. During the latter part of this ministry I tried many times to evaluate how well my work was going. I had started some new programs in religious studies, worship, and service and had decided to continue other programs without change. So it was natural that I wanted very much to know (in my less defensive moments) whether the way I had chosen to minister was better than the alternatives I had rejected along the way. What was working and what was not? What should be continued and what ought to be dropped? Few forms of ministry today afford so delightful an opportunity to influence and observe changes in spiritual growth as a four-year residential school chaplaincy, yet I found myself unable to draw useful conclusions from my experience.

Plenty of Results But . . .

This was not for lack of results. I knew which approaches produced the most interest in the Bible and which taught the most biblical knowledge. I could sense whether a sermon was theologically sound and whether it was liked by the students. I kept figures on student participation in every "religious" activity sponsored by the school. Yet when it came to using these results to evaluate a year's ministry, I was unable to find theologically significant meaning in any of this information. The results could be evaluated pedagogically, psychologically, or administratively with some degree of competence. But to assume that all this somehow added up to an evaluation of ministerial effectiveness seemed to me—and still does—sheer presumption.

. . . How Do You Tell?

The question for me was simply: "How can I make a theologically informed judgment about the worth of this ministry?" My feeling was that if there is no *reliable* way to determine success or failure of a ministry—in even the most elemental theological sense—then such a ministry can hardly be called a profession. Professional judgments require a far clearer picture (than that possessed by most ministers) of what "good" and "bad" results look like. Ministerial training in the seminaries has yet to take the problem seriously, and ministerial experience is often a blind guide. Nowhere could I find a simple, straightforward description of the desired—and expected—results of a competent ministry. It was then that I realized I wouldn't know a Christian if I saw one.

In the years since this awful truth hit home, I have found others struggling with the same problem. Some are ministers, some are laymen, but all share an underlying uneasiness with this void in professional knowledge. They know that the mature Christian life is qualitatively different from the life untouched by the power of Christ's redeeming grace but are at a loss to say exactly what this difference is. To them one person often looks like another, Christian or pagan. They are weary of hearing theologians extol the difference without helping them to know whether Mr. Jones is a mature Christian or an unregenerate pagan. Knowing the concrete shape of the Christian life is crucial. Too long it has been the misty vanishing point, not the starting point, for the work of the church. This book is for those who like myself can no longer in good conscience attempt to "do" the work of the church without some reliable way of telling whether they are doing it well or poorly.

chapter I

TELLING THE SHEEP
FROM THE GOATS

I

Who Is a Christian?

Of all the challenges that face Christianity today, it may seem odd to suggest that the greatest is discovering who is a Christian and who is not.

At first impression this can be a distressing allegation—if not a patent oversimplification, then certainly an invitation to another Inquisition! In these days of growing ecumenical concern and new awareness of the social complexities facing Christianity, so simple a view is immediately suspect. But the guiding presupposition of everything to follow is that Christianity can fare no better on earth or in heaven than her ability to tell the sheep from the goats.

Something like Medical Quackery?

An illustration from a related field may help to put this into proper perspective. Imagine the future of medicine if it could not distinguish a healthy person from an unhealthy one! Within a matter of years it would be reduced to general health cures, patent medicines, and quack practitioners. Learned medical treatises would still be published on the general principles of health and disease, but of what benefit would they be if even their author could not apply these principles to a patient? In the general confusion the healthy would be called sick and the sick healthy.

Imagine also what might happen if a doctor never knew whether a particular treatment worked or not. Lacking reliable knowledge of how similar treatments had fared and having no way to check the worth of a current course of treatment, the modern medical practitioner would have less to offer than a witch doctor. His assuring "This will be good for you" would have about as much meaning as it has today when the authority is a minister, the subject is spiritual health, and the proposed treatment is church-going.

But Medicine Has Changed

Despite its obvious limitations, the analogy between physical health and spiritual health is a fascinating one because of the numerous ties they possess. For many centuries they ran parallel courses, both defining the cure by the treatment chosen—and not the treatment by the cure effected. There are exceptions, it is true. No matter how deductive his approach, the doctor has always had his set of rough empirical bench marks. Yet we smile at the saying, "The operation was a success but the patient died," recognizing the lingering propensity in medical thought to confuse means with ends. The saying is humorous because we realize that were medicine to be practiced without taking notice of results, there would soon be a vast gulf between these results and its aims. But tragically this is the way Christianity has been practiced from the beginning. Why is this so? Scripture states explicitly that "you will know them by their fruits." [1] Then from whence comes this alarming unconcern for examining results in the practice of spiritual health?

Why the Ministry Remained "Unprofessional"

The simple truth is that theologians learned to avoid the issue after repeated failure to define and identify the fruits of the Christian life.[2] They then began to devise various "formulas" by which, supposedly, such results could be *inferred* from things more easily identified. Far from profiting from the tortuous tangle of scholastic reasoning that resulted, the Protestant reformers themselves fell headlong into formulizing the very heart of their principal contribution, justification by faith. It is only as we focus upon a sample Protestant formula, making explicit its various terms, that we begin to understand what went wrong and what now must be done to remedy the situation.

Protestantism's "Hidden Formula"

The central claim of the New Testament heralded in Protestant theology might be stated as follows: if the (1) *gospel* is (2) *preached* and (3) *believed,* the consequence is (4) *new life in Christ.* Traditionally, the Protestant church and her theologians have assumed that the natures of elements 1, 2, and 3 of this "formula" determine the nature of element 4—the new life in Christ. Since it has remained the singular predicament of the Protestant church never to have concretely defined the new life in Christ, it is not surprising that so many doctrinal disagreements have grown up around the meaning and the emphases given to the gospel, preaching, and believing.

Purify the Gospel!

Protestant traditions emphasizing "Bible-centered," "gospel-centered," or "content-centered" approaches of the more literalistic kind tend to focus upon the *gospel* element. If we contend with the fundamentailst theologian J. G. Machen that "the lives of men are transformed by a piece of news," [3] we are likely to insist that this Good News be jealously guarded against possible contamination. And if we further claim that the written and spoken Word itself contains quasi-magical properties ensuring "vital contact with Jesus," [4] it is understandable how we might lean toward some rather strict rules for defining and using the gospel. The hallmark of the fundamentalist tradition is its obsession with eliminating ambiguity from the gospel element of the formula.

The Pulpit as the Key

More central to the reformed Protestant tradition is an emphasis upon the second, or *preaching*, element of the formula. Here the gospel is no less important, but the focus is upon how it is interpreted and preached. The gospel has no power to communicate itself. To transform the lives of men it must be preached with conviction and understanding. It comes alive in the preacher's struggle to fathom the meaning of the written word as it touches his life and the lives of his congregation. For this reason we find the reformed Protestant tradition stressing both the scholarly interpretation of scripture and the art of preaching. Gospel and believing are not slighted;[5] it is the gospel that is preached so that men may believe. By virtue of its long neglect, however, informed and inspired preaching assumed critical importance to those who saw it becoming the weak link in the chain of events leading to the new life in Christ.

The Cult of Belief

The presumption that *believing* merely "follows" from what happens in the pulpit or at the altar is disputed by those who emphasize the third element of the formula. Christian existentialists, pietists, creedalists, and secularists, while differing in other important respects, share a common concern for the inner convictions of the Christian. Some lay more stress on what is believed, others on how it is believed. But all feel that the gospel and its proclamation have little consequence for Christian life unless they engender a lively belief in the hearer. These Protestants suggest that if true belief can be established, the first two elements of the formula may be assumed and the last confidently predicted. Whatever the signs of belief—whether creedal confession, good works, "ultimate concern," conversion, or certain inward feelings—identifying criteria are sooner or later evolved to permit constant surveillance of this key to the Christian life.

A Shoddy Method Gives Shoddy Results

It is of little importance whether extreme instances of the gospel, preaching, and believing emphases can be found. In every Christian tradition and theology, denomination and local church, some combination of these three occurs. Even to emphasize all three equally would not relieve the essential problem posed by this illustration—for to emphasize any or all of these first three elements of the formula is to make a claim regarding the fourth element, *new life in Christ*. It is saying, in effect, that following a certain method ensures this result and deviation from it does not. It is to become bound by our own "methodism" and split into opposing denominations and sects. But worst of all it is to presume that there is no identifiable shape to the Christian life.

Is There a Better Way?

Consider now what would happen if a way were found to define and identify mature Christian life *independently* of any such religious formula or method. For one thing, we could distinguish various levels of Christian maturity among individuals and groups. That would make it possible to distinguish between effective and ineffective religious methods. Christian growth would no longer be an accidental, hit-or-miss affair. Like physical health, it could be planned for by adopting the particular "treatment" found most effective in similar situations. At the very least, it would allow you and me to identify the shape of the Christian life with enough skill to make possible an informed appraisal of Mr. Jones' growth in the Christian life. It is this more modest goal that forms the immediate objective of the next five chapters.

The Spiritual Hunch—Sharp but Unreliable

No doubt there are persons who already possess this skill. Experienced ministers oftentimes report a cultivated sixth sense for identifying signs of spiritual health. In the presence of an individual or group, they have a "feeling" of the situation. Without being able to explain why, they know whether or not the Spirit is at work.

There is every reason to believe that such practiced intuition and experienced judgment is genuine. That there exist among us observers whose spiritual intuition far exceeds the possibilities of that which is to be proposed in these pages is not disputed. The point is only that if there are such men, we have no way of telling who they are. For every person who possesses the ability there may be ten who are convinced they do but actually do not. No way has been found to evaluate the evaluators.

The basic weakness of identification by intuition is that

it relies on distortable inner processes which operate outside our conscious knowledge and control. For this reason the frequently invoked analogy between the seasoned minister and the experienced sea captain is a poor one. The captain's practiced intuition in foretelling stormy weather functions with a built-in check; when he is wrong, he soon learns his mistake. The predicament of the minister is that he seldom learns from his mistakes because he seldom knows when he makes one. Without the possibility of comparing cultivated intuition with reliable bench marks, there is little hope for arresting or detecting cumulative errors in judgment.

II

Beginning a Better Way

If not by intuition, then how can we judge a man's spiritual health—his degree of Christian maturity—*independently* of Protestantism's shaky formula? The answer proposed by this book is a basically simple one: take from the theologian his picture of the life of faith and apply it to the man in the pew. How good is the fit?

Simple as it sounds, judging the fit can be dangerous business without a disciplined way to do it—disciplined in the way the picture is extracted and disciplined in the way it is applied to living persons. Something of how these two tasks may be accomplished will conclude the chapter.

How to See People While Reading Theology

First we must derive a faithful picture of Christian life from centuries of Protestant thought! A computer might do it, but the mind is a keener instrument—if it has a method. Our method for describing the shape of the Christian life grows out of behavioral expectations in traditional Protestant theology. It consists of nothing more than calling attention to those expectations that are explicitly stated and making explicit those that are implied. In this volume five characteristics of the mature Christian life found in representative Protestant thought are described. Contrasting examples of each behavioral characteristic are presented in the context of the situations that most often elicit them.[6] The idea is to make possible an unambiguous mental picture of each characteristic, a picture resembling in form and clarity the type of "clinical" description found in casebook studies of a well-defined mental illness.

Such vividness of description is of little worth, however, if it cannot be shown that the five characteristics are, in fact, rooted in Protestant thought. This is not a treatise on mental health, but on Christian behavior. The task of justifying the use of the term "Protestant" can only be begun here, for to consider every notable Protestant theologian since the Reformation would be a staggering undertaking. Nevertheless, a feeling for how Protestant thought describes the mature Christian life in terms of these five behavioral characteristics can be grasped from the views of leading theologians footnoted in this volume.

Where Christ Is at Work

The term "mature Christian life" itself is rarely found in theological literature. Among the more familiar religious concepts informing the use of this term are the "Christian life," the "life of faith," "life in the Spirit," "spiritual health," "new life," and the "redeemed life in Christ." Some of these have already been used to speak of mature Christian life. Despite the broad range of synonyms, the essential meaning of the term has considerable conceptual clarity. The mature Christian life is the life in which Christ is at work and the life in which this work of redemption has taken hold. As such, it is a life which shows forth the "fruits of the Spirit" in full maturity, not simply in an early stage of development.

The Long-List Trap

To establish a person's degree of Christian maturity from only five areas of behavior may seem a bit risky. Are there not other qualities required of the mature Christian life? Obviously yes. A list a page long could be compiled using only those characteristics of mature Christian life mentioned by the theologians cited in this volume. Some would be behaviors; others would be feelings, convictions, and similar inward experiences. Were one to view Christian life as consisting of so many qualities or characteristics, it could be inferred only that a person could *not* be a mature Christian if he lacked some quality deemed necessary for Christian life.

This "negative argument" is the basis of Paul's well-known discourse on love in the thirteenth chapter of First Corinthians. The approach can be of real value when the absence of a vital quality can be established. Yet Paul would be the first to object if love became the sole criterion for the Christian life, a master virtue. By means of the negative argument the best that can be said of any such quality or characteristic is that it is a necessary (and not sufficient) condition of mature Christian life. This implies the somewhat disconcerting conclusion that it is easier to tell who is not a mature Christian than who is a mature Christian.

The Behavior of Grace

A more dynamic view of Protestant thought can help to remove this logical and practical difficulty. If we do not begin with a list of Christian qualities or characteristics but with an understanding of grace as it transforms human lives, we are driven to acknowledge a number of functional priorities for mature Christian life. The main one is a freeing sense of security. Without this, faith turns to works. No Christian understanding of grace active in human life is compatible with the person who has long been without this freeing sense of security. To the degree that a person lacks it, he is not free to think, feel, and act as a mature Christian; to the degree that a person possesses this sense of security, it enables every Christian quality and characteristic found in Protestant thought. For this reason it is the *conditio sine qua non* of the mature Christian life and will be considered first (Chapter II).

The Freedom to Do or Not to Do

Genuine Christian "behavior" is not primarily to be understood in terms of what a person does, or even what he means to do, but by what he is *able* to do. The Christian is one who has the freedom to do or not to do. He possesses abilities lacking in others. Four types of abilities predominate: he is able to know himself without deception (Chapter III), to express himself honestly (Chapter IV), to perceive the world without distortion (Chapter V), and to fully respond to its demands upon him (Chapter VI). A brief definition of these characteristics appears in the adjoining diagram.

It will be seen that the four "ability" characteristics bear a certain relationship to one another and to a freeing sense of security. It is this basic sense of security that enables the four types of behavior. The relationship also presupposes that at least one of these four characteristics is the key dynamic underlying every area of mature Christian life. In short, we are assuming that a freeing sense of security has four distinguishable expressions and can be behaviorally identified by them.

A Freeing Sense of Security (Chapter II) To live with the kind of inner freedom, both normally and in the face of threat or uncertainty, that has no need to distort or manipulate life to make it seem more secure.		
Passive Modality ("perceiving . . .")	Self-knowledge (Chapter III) The ability to recognize and acknowledge as one's own those past and present thoughts, feelings, and acts which most deeply affect one's life.	Accurate Perception (Chapter V) The ability to perceive the world as it is, to have a sensitive awareness of others' lives, and to be open to all kinds of experience.
Active Modality ("responding to . . .")	Honest Expression (Chapter IV) The ability to express one's desires, feelings thoughts, and doubts naturally and without fear.	Adequate Response (Chapter VI) The ability to respond in a way appropriate to the nature and occasion of that which is experienced, adopting behavioral patterns not rigidly bound by personal scruples or social expectations.
	Subjective Perspective (. . . oneself")	Objective Perspective (. . . the world")

How It All Fits Together

Self-knowledge and honest expression constitute a "subjective" perspective by which one's sense of security may be viewed, while accurate perception and adequate response comprise its "objective" expression. In the former two the emphasis is upon the ability to know oneself and to be able to express oneself in an honest and forthright manner when the situation warrants. Sense of security viewed from an objective perspective stresses the ability to perceive the world as it is (and others as they are) and to respond appropriately. In essence the subjective perspective is concerned with a person's perception and response to that which is within himself, and the objective perspective is concerned with a person's perception and response to the social and natural world in which he lives.

Conceptualized a different way, a freeing sense of security adds another dimension defined by "active" and "passive" modalities. Self-knowledge and accurate perception relate to abilities having a more passive character. Both point to perceptual abilities, that of perceiving oneself accurately and of perceiving the world accurately. Complementing this is the active modality which includes the two "response" abilities designated by honest expression and adequate response. Both are concerned with appropriateness of response, one to internal events and the other to external events.

Rooted in Human Experience

Apart from these structural differences, self-knowledge, honest expression, accurate perception, and adequate response are well-defined concepts in human experience. Long before anyone thought of arranging them neatly in structural models, they were deemed distinctive forms of behavior. Doubtlessly these four characteristics precondition thought and language about human experience. Both the theoretical and empirical study of human behavior have gained conceptual clarity by recognizing a certain "givenness" about them.

For example, the theologian often contrasts revelation and ethics in a manner similar to the way the observant man in the street contrasts accurate perception with adequate response. The psychologist may see the same differences (in negative form) between what he calls perceptual defense or denial and rigid or compulsive reaction. As native students of human behavior, we all seem to follow the same pattern in speaking, thinking, and organizing behavioral characteristics. In this sense both form and content of the clinical-type descriptions of human behavior to follow are more likely to be basic to Protestant thought than simply imposed upon it.

A Practical Purpose

While this volume should be of interest to those wanting to understand the dynamics of Christian life in commonplace, nontechnical, and "secular" terms, it is written with a more practical purpose in mind. With the possibility of reliably distinguishing between persons and groups on the basis of Christian maturity comes the opportunity for making informed judgments about the value of any institution or program that claims to aid in Christian growth. This should have immediate appeal for ministers and Christian educators who have professional responsibilities in this area. But it is no less important a concern for Christian laymen or for persons who cannot honestly embrace institutional Christianity on merely the hope or promise that it can help them attain Christian maturity. This volume is based on the premise that there is no substitute for reliable knowledge as a worthy guide to Christian growth. The purpose of the volume is to suggest a means of establishing a few bench marks along the way.

The clinical-type descriptions that form the core of each of the following five chapters are but the first step toward this goal. Hopefully they may provide enough conceptual clarity to permit identification of relatively pronounced instances of Christian maturity and immaturity. In the hands of an experienced and sensitive observer of human behavior, these descriptions can check and sharpen intuitive judgment. Other means for identifying Christian maturity, like those mentioned in the final chapter, can be tested as well. But it is wise to recognize a limit to the usefulness of informal observation. It is only the most immediate possibility suggested by the clinical-type descriptions to follow.

Sharpening Up the Picture to Fit the Person

Greater accuracy in identification, especially in instances where differences are not extreme, requires more than a method of matching behavioral descriptions with actual instances of behavior. Judgments concerning growth in Christian life compound this difficulty by requiring "before" and "after" comparisons as well as controlled observation.

In light of these difficulties, a final section of each of the next five chapters suggests how a few selected empirical tests and experimental designs can significantly strengthen the reliability of both identification and growth estimates. For only when judgments can be quantified, spurious influences controlled, intended influences measured, and results subjected to statistical analysis, can we speak of the production of reliable knowledge. The final section of each of these chapters may be viewed as an invitation to further a theologically and empirically disciplined study of Christian growth.

III

Before You Turn the Page

If you have come to the end of this chapter unready to go on, do one of the following: read it again or turn to the final chapter—there you will find discussed some of the basic issues that underlie both the "problem" and the "solution" sections of this chapter. A feeling for the problem is needed to find much value in the rest of the book. If your unreadiness takes the form of quiet rage with the nature of the solution proposed, the final chapter may ease a few objections.

Yet a mild degree of confusion and irritation is not without value at this point. Things will get clearer, not by talking abstractly about them, but by diving in.

NOTES

1. Matt. 7:16.

2. A few of the more important attempts to define and identify the fruits of the Christian life are mentioned in Chapter VII (pp. 173-77), along with some of the reasons why these attempts probably failed.

3. J. Gresham Machen, *Christianity and Liberalism* (New York: Macmillan, 1923), p. 48.

4. *Ibid.*, p. 42.

5. There is no intention to minimize the importance of the sacraments in the reformed tradition. For the sake of simplicity they have not been included in the "formula." In many ways sacramental emphasis provides the most striking example of a means assumed to assure an end.

6. For the sake of conceptual clarity and faithfulness to theological sources, the contrasting examples of behavioral characteristics are portrayed as ideal types. They represent extreme ends of the continuum between mature Christian life and its opposite. Rarely, if ever, will they describe an actual person. What the contrasting ideal types describe are the characteristics toward which actual persons tend. A mature Christian is someone who, in relation to others and to his own potential, more closely approaches the positive ideal type.

—————————chapter II—————————

A CHRISTIAN IS SOMEONE WHO CAN LEAVE HOME

(Without Taking the Furniture with Him)

I

Knowledge of Divine Favor

The heart of the Protestant tradition finds its clearest expression in the doctrine of justification by faith. The doctrine has many meanings, but one stands above the rest. This is the claim that God accepts us as we are. *Why* this is so and *how* this happens are of secondary importance. For Protestant thought the simple conviction *that* God is faithful expresses the deepest faith of Christian man.

Who Is a Man of Faith?

If this insight has been Protestantism's singular triumph, the inability to identify so simple a human conviction has proved its most serious weakness. Who is the man that is inwardly convinced of God's faithfulness? Who is a man of faith? It is often assumed that the inwardness of faith can be identified by what a man believes or confesses. Common sense tells us that Christian belief and confession, even when sincere, may be prompted by unrecognized inward needs and may indicate nothing more than self-deception. There is also some question as to whether belief and confession (as commonly understood) are necessary to Christian faith as Protestantism sees it. Add to this the difficulties raised by such purported "outward signs of inward grace" as the virtues, the marks and signs of the church, etc., and the dimensions of this Protestant predicament may be grasped.

Faith and Thinking, Faith and Knowledge

The predicament is avoided if we relinquish one assumption: that genuine faith has mostly to do with thinking. The assumption runs deep in Protestant thought. We are reminded of John Calvin's classic definition of faith as a "firm and sure knowledge of the divine favour toward us." [1] It is true that Calvin could not conceive of "knowledge" apart from the act of thinking, but it would be unrealistic to claim that this was all he meant. For every Protestant theologian steeped in the Scriptures, knowledge of God is prior to thinking. Knowledge is a perception, an awareness of that which can more readily be experienced than made the object of thought. Thinking is the way man seeks to label, master, and communicate such knowledge. The man of faith is one who perceives God's faithfulness toward him at the most fundamental level of human experience. Thinking may sharpen or distort this perception of God's faithfulness. Thinking may help him to symbolize, recall, reflect on, or talk about the perception, or it may not. But thinking is not knowing. It has a different function.

Because a "firm and sure knowledge" need not be a conceptually clear and articulate knowledge, it cannot be reliably identified by the content and quality of a man's religious beliefs, confessions, or other mental acts mediated by conscious thought. What is required is a means of identifying faith that takes into account a considerably broader range of human response to an awareness of "divine favour toward us." H. Richard Niebuhr provides a clue to what this might be when he describes the man of faith as one who in every sphere of his life assumes that "there is a faithfulness at the heart of things." [2]

The Sense of God's Faithfulness

To know the God who justifies and accepts one is first of all to sense *an* underlying faithfulness about life itself—a faithfulness beyond the experience of those who are continually unfaithful and unaccepting. To sense *a* faithfulness at the heart of things can only mean that one senses *God's* faithfulness toward him, since Protestant thought is abundantly clear that only God can grant this "peace that passes all understanding." This is a crucial theological insight, but a poor test of faith. There is no reason why every person who experiences God's faithfulness should believe or claim it to be God's faithfulness.

Writing Between the Lines

In spite of the basic confusion between the demands of theology and the demands of faith reflected in Protestant thought, Protestant theologians are to be credited with a great sensitivity to the human dimensions of the doctrine of justification by faith. After describing the man of faith in terms of traditionally "religious" beliefs, confession, feelings, and behavior, the insightful work begins. From the heart of a theologian's struggle with the meaning of faith for human life often comes a wonderfully refreshing view of the man of faith. Orthodox or liberal, dated or contemporary, it makes no difference which theologian is selected. If he is a truly great theologian, he will find some opportunity to describe Christian faith as he sees it in himself and in the lives of those around him. The following pages attempt to summarize some of these insights.

II

The Man of Faith: A Personal Profile

Sensing Solid Ground

The man of faith in Protestant thought seems to be the kind of person who has an abiding sense of security in fair or foul weather, an almost childlike "undoubting confidence." [3] He senses a certainty in life, something unconditional yet caring, as a child feels the security of his "father's house" or his "mother's lap." [4] He is aware of being grounded in something ultimate, enduring, and unshakable. He can "feel at home" in the world. Whether it is friendly or hostile, he finds "comfort" in its midst.[5] This may be felt as a delight and joy in all things, a lifting hope, a sense of blessedness and peace. Beneath each feeling lies a basic "sense of security." Change and adversity serve only to occasion the awareness of "solid ground . . . under his feet." [6]

"In Spite of" Acceptance

Closely allied is the feeling of being accepted. Such acceptance has an "in spite of" quality. The man of faith feels accepted in full and painful knowledge of his unacceptable deeds. He knows the security of the child able to offer his parents works that are "only begun or half finished, or even with something faulty in them." [7] He senses a meaning to his life beyond his inadequacies and failures, a cosmic concern for him, as though a voice were saying: "You are accepted. *You are accepted,* accepted by that which is greater than you, and the name of which you do not know. Do not ask for the name now; perhaps you will find it later. Do not try to do anything now; perhaps you will do much. Do not seek for anything; do not perform anything; do not intend anything. *Simply accept the fact that you are accepted"* [8]

Feeling accepted, he is able to accept himself. He holds a good opinion of himself without having to think of something else. Business success, athletic prowess, or academic proficiency do not affect the way he sees his worth. Wipe these away, and he thinks no less of himself. As a Christian he is perhaps surprised and interested to discover a Jewish relative, but not threatened. As a white Southerner he feels no differently about himself upon learning of a Negro ancestor. He loses and gains social standing, money, admiration, and health with regret and elation but little change in the way he views his "significance and value [as] a person." [9] The man of faith has his goals and ambitions in life and may work toward them with a consuming passion. But when others forge ahead to score the touchdowns, he accepts it without bitterness or self-pity, perhaps even smiling at his own Walter Mitty pretensions. There is no situation that can make him feel more or less a person.

Self-acceptance means also that he is free to be himself. The man of faith feels no need to make an impression on anyone. He can accept or reject an offer of friendship, depending upon how the person strikes him. He is the same with VIPs as with has-beens, with peers as with family. His likes and dislikes are hidden only as discretion demands, nor does he fear how people regard him. To overhear a derogatory remark or a critical comment may hurt, but it does not shake him. He can see himself through the eyes of others and understand their feelings about him without threat. In the company of others he can forget about the spot on his tie, the scar on his cheek, or the way he speaks. Nor is he known to lose sleep reliving each encounter with sharper comebacks or besting remarks.[10]

The same unassuming confidence is seen at home. Family life may be far from harmonious but is not overlaid with layers of "pretension."[11] The man of faith is unashamed to be human. His children respect him as a father without believing he is always right. He allows his wife to see him fail and make mistakes. There are no subtle games to assert his authority in the family circle, since his authority is a natural expression of his sense of worth. Whether at home or at work, with those who know him best or least, he finds he does not have to act like a god to feel like a man.[12]

By the same measure that he accepts himself, the man of faith is able to accept others. Aware of the splinter in his own eye, he is not offended by the beam in his brother's. He finds it easy to trust others when trust is warranted. He is able to depend upon others without constant assurances of their trustworthiness. He will accept the criticism of a friend without suspecting betrayal and the affection of his wife without demanding "proofs." If he trusts his children, he will respect their right to run risks and make mistakes. When circumstances indicate their lack of judgment or strength, he imposes the necessary restrictions and discipline in a way that strengthens the bond of trust between them. Betrayal of trust itself, be it by stranger, friend, or relation, is a personal loss occasioned more by disappointment and sadness than by distrust of others. Although he has learned "never to trust a scoundrel an inch," he is able to give himself "to the trustworthy without reserve."[13]

At Home in the Unknown

So pervasive is this sense of trusting that he is quite at home on "unknown ground." He has a "readiness for the

34

unknown future." No deep terror lurks beneath the surface of the new, the strange, and the dark. From earliest infancy he senses the world to be trustworthy.[14] Noises in the night and Halloween witches are spooky, but fun spooky. The first day of school is bewildering, but exciting too. Away from home for the first time at camp or in military service, he is perhaps homesick and appalled by the strangeness of it all, but eager also to try his new wings.

And so on into his mature years. Nothing is spared him, not even the emptiness of failure or the burden of grief. Daily he is confronted by his own limitations. He is surpassed by younger men, often confused by his children, and disappointed by himself. Yet he lives in the present, secure in the knowledge that he can "stand the loss of . . . possession, . . . name, . . . life, and everything else." Beset by afflictions, uncertainties, and frustrations, he is not unconcerned, but manages to ride out the storm without losing his sense of perspective.[15] He himself may be surprised by the way disappointment and tragedy often bring their legacy of confidence, and even hope.

In this way the man of faith combines the rare ability "to feel at home" in the world and yet free from its anxious concerns. He cherishes life, the big things and the small, what lies ahead and what is at hand, and yet he could "give up everything, let it go" if the occasion demanded, with no more than appropriate regret. He may come to fear many things, but his sense of security is such that he is also "free not to fear." [16]

Abraham—Just "Going"

If there is one quality above all others that distinguishes the man of faith, it is the ability to leave home. It seems likely that Abraham is known as the Father of Faith for just this reason. The writer of the Letter to the Hebrews tells us: "By faith Abraham obeyed when he was called to go out to a place which he was to receive as an inheritance; and he went out, not knowing where he was to go." [17] The story of Abraham in the book of Genesis begins with this impression: "Now the Lord said to Abram, 'Go from your country and your kindred and your father's house to the land that I will show you.' . . . So Abram went. . . .'" [18]

As the misty figure of Abraham meets us from out of the past, it is simply his "going" that strikes us as extraordinary. It is of no little importance that he believed in God and obeyed his command, but this he had in common with a host of other biblical figures who are not known as the Father of Faith. To set out into the unknown, to leave the familiar for the unfamiliar, is difficult enough in these days of rootless mobility. But to go "from your father's house" in the time of Abraham can only have meant an act of ultimate human freedom.[19]

Abraham went into the unknown when he set out from Ur of the Chaldees. All he had for security were a few vague promises concerning the prosperity of his descendants. He did it again when he went into Egypt and again when he set off into the wilderness of Moriah to sacrifice the one person who could guarantee his posthumous security, Issac. The Bible tells little of Abraham's seeking after assurances to make the way more familiar and bearable, as did Moses, David, Solomon, and the prophets. From all appearances Abraham seems to have been that rare sort of person who can face the unknown without something to prop him up, the person who has the kind of freedom to take things as they come without fearing the unexpected.

With Abraham it is no longer necessary to speak of faith in terms of a basic sense of security, a feeling of being accepted, trust, and the rest. All this is presumed. It comes together in the one remarkable ability to leave home. No true appraisal of human experience could maintain that an

Abraham can leave home in the biblically protrayed sense without having a profound awareness of already *being* at home in the world. Through what divine or human agency this awareness comes to man is of crucial religious and psychological importance but is not the issue here. Whatever the cause, the essence of Christian maturity itself is best expressed by this radical freedom to act, the freedom to leave home in *every* sphere—emotional, religious, social, economic, etc.—of one's life. It is this ability to "let goods and kindred go, this mortal life also" [20] that seems most clearly to identify the justified man in Protestant thought.

The Man of Little Faith

A Child of Untrustworthiness

By way of contrast theologians describe a person whose every attitude and action seem to reflect an untrustworthy world, as though some deep "fear of the unknown" had him in its grasp. He is like an unwanted baby who has known the sudden panic of hunger, the terror of surprise, or the despair of utter loneliness. Whatever the outward expression, he carries in his heart a "secret dread" of what life may bring. His world invites only "skeptical" doubt, a corrosive, cynical, despairing doubt.[21] He is inwardly unsure of everything: his abilities, his worth as a person, his acceptability to others, the trustworthiness of friends, and the intentions of the world. Despite a "yearning for security," he has a radical distrust of "any certainty." He gropes desperately for solid rock but knows that it will only turn to sand at the touch. He feels as though "everything is uncertain in the whole circle of his experience." [22] For him, fear, distrust, and the unfamiliar are of one piece as if the only world that he knew were a punishing, uncaring, and arbitrary one.

He May Show It Openly . . .

Such feelings are difficult to hide. Both crisis and friendship, if unexpected, may cause him to speak openly of these feelings. Or he may evidence them by his actions. For example, his fears may be acted out in a pervasive distrust of those closest to him or by a suspicion of a person's traits, beliefs, class, and race that appear to differ from his. Whatever the fear that has a "secret hold upon him," he "tries to impose it on other people." He may also show signs of "harrassing care" in an anxiousness, apprehensiveness, and sense of desperation in everything he does. By whatever standard, his feelings and acts are patently "disproportionate" to the degree of actual threat he faces.[23]

. . . Or Try to Hide It

More likely, however, the man of little faith will not show himself so openly. To know oneself as afraid, depressed, distrustful, or anxious is not a pleasant thing. To be known as such flatters no one. And so he may be driven to "build . . . a city and tower with its top in the heavens" and like the men of old "make a name" for himself lest his true name be known. He tries to build a more certain, predictable, and familiar world to wall out fear. He is Peter beholding the Transfiguration and desiring to "make three booths," or the man who bid Jesus divide an inheritance that had no division.[24] His feeling of safety hinges precariously on how well he can "make a distinction" where little exists. Deprived of the opportunity for being certain or maintaining differences in one area of life, he clutches for other supports, something "observable and calculable." Definiteness in any form becomes a sanctuary to be built at all costs.[25]

When building is an escape from fear, two paths may be chosen. One makes things familiar by forcing the world into a familiar mold. Another keeps things familiar by re-treating into an imaginary world. Both seek to minimize the possibility of the unexpected.

Remaking the World: The Path of Works-Righteousness

Along the first path the man of little faith will assume an active posture against the world. He thrusts himself into human affairs in order to understand, control, and manipulate them. He is like David, desperately attempting to use people and events to preserve his popular image.[26] By exploiting others he achieves a sense of mastery. His gaze misses few signs of human weakness that can be turned to personal gain—a "mistrustful surveillance and appraisal of everything." He is often hard-working, hardheaded, and successful in worldly affairs, his inner doubt and despair finding expression in a cynical realism. The life he hammers out is not his own, but the denial of every weakness, fear, and uncertainty that haunts him. To exorcise these demons he strives to make his mark on the world, the familiar and definite mark of human accomplishment. On the hard face of reality he seeks to stamp this counterfeit image and likeness of himself.[27]

Such a person compels the respect of others to assure his own self-respect. Behind his efforts after self-sufficiency and self-glorification is a "spiritually sick need for the admiration of men." By the works of his hands he hopes to capture and bind the respect of the world: the more impressive the accomplishment, the more certain the respect.[28] He runs a faster mile, builds a longer bridge, drives a harder bargain, gives a bigger donation, writes a more beautiful sonnet, or works longer hours. He "must achieve something." Whatever is achieved, there is a "desperate clinging to one's own goodness" in the face of lingering uncertainties and doubts that involve this accomplishment in "the vicious circle of accentuating the insecurity which it intends to eliminate." [29]

The Leaner Within the Pusher

No matter how aggressive and forceful a face he turns toward the world, this person is inordinately dependent upon other people. He scans the social spectrum for signs of approval or rebuke. He will "look right and left for results." All humanity comes under his calculating eye, including his own; for he must control himself as well as others if the unexpected is to be avoided and the brittle image maintained. Although he may vanquish the world, he is continually engaged in "secret listening" for the world's judgment of himself.[30] When he senses the threat of disapproval, he attempts to turn the situation to his advantage. Like a desperate child seeking the affection of his parents, he may smile, submit, obey, cling to others, or appear passive so that others will like and admire him. Whatever will manipulate approval, bring things into line with his desires and expectations, and force the world into a familiar mold is done with predictable regularity. Yet, ironically, when he perceives just this approval and certainty, his pervading sense of unworthiness cheats him of its promised benefits. "Always in doubt," he never knows "peace of heart." [31] This is the path of *works-righteousness*.

Withdrawing from the World: The Path of Fantasy

The second path leads to illusion. If the man of little faith cannot change the world to suit his conception, he will retreat from the world in order to lessen the risk that it may change his conception. He learns to see things the way he wants to see them. The more the outer world differs from his expectations the more he must "take refuge" in inner worlds of thought and fantasy. Rather than seeking after little assurances to make the way more familiar and bearable, he creates them. "Wishful thinking" takes form in the "construction of imaginary worlds." [32] His world assumes the familiar structure of his desires. He plans for the future, reconstructs the past, and sees the present in terms of his "vain imagination." All this he can do in the name of novelty without risking its actual threat since he believes he can "complete the structure of truth from within." [33]

A Lonely Loner

Such a person often seems detached and aloof. He shows little "capacity for imagination and feeling" toward the drama of life that swirls around him until some piece of it happens to touch an emotionally charged piece of his fantasy world. At these times he may be catapulted into momentary activity and feeling totally inappropriate to the occasioning event.[34] With only these outbursts punctuating an otherwise withdrawn, listless, and shallow emotional life, he gives the impression of a neglected and lonely three-year-old. A catchy tune or lively beat usually leaves him unaffected. He is generally unconcerned about his dress or personal appearance, the food that he eats and the events of the day—although he may affect a bizarre interest in them at times. Games, competition, sex, and humor often seem to frighten him, eliciting either indifference or stiff acknowledgment. However interesting the face he shows to the world, underneath he is a dull and colorless individual. His response to the world is "merely an urge outwards, an indefinite agility without form or color." [35]

His escape from reality may be most apparent in his social relations. He is usually a loner. People do not seem to interest him; he forms only superficial emotional attachments without possibility for "real communication" or mean-ingful "self-giving." Those who attempt to befriend him are often met with suspicion, or at best, passive acceptance. Since he is unable to love or accept love, "to know others or . . . to be known by them," rarely does marriage bring him—or his partner—any satisfaction. His relationships are characteristic-ally cold, distant, and formal, as though he feared getting too close to anyone.[36]

Paradoxically, he often nurses a strong desire for personal intimacy and acutely senses the feelings of others toward him. His "dream world" is peopled with lovers and admirers constant in their devotion to him. Despite his generally distorted view of reality, he may quite accurately perceive the inconstancy and pretense of the affection people offer. He fears their rejection, not real affection. People regard him as odd, and he knows it. His response is not to remove the oddness, but to remove himself from those who see him as odd. "Running away from himself" means moving apart from others.[37]

In such a situation simple communication and effective-ness are often seriously impaired. It is difficult for him to to put into words his thoughts and feelings in ways under-standable to another or to be in "open perception of the other." For this reason he often maintains a stony silence or expresses himself in terse stereotypes. He prefers reading or solitary activities to being with people and sometimes achieves a degree of eminence in tasks rewarding skill and perseverance in these areas. He may be a gifted artist or inventor, a responsible night watchman or elevator operator. But more often than not his preference for "illusion" and "escape from . . . reality" make him unproductive and im-practical in all worldly affairs. Although generally unhappy, he prefers the familiarity of fantasy to the uncertainty of life.[38] This is the path of *illusion*.

Both Paths Seek a False Security

Regardless of which path is chosen, works-righteousness or illusion, it is an effort to "impose upon reality a law which is alien to it." [39] This person cannot tolerate the normal ambiguities of life. He maintains his sense of well-being and security only so long as he is not confronted with the unknown. To find safety is to find the familiar, the predictable, and the controllable. Take away all the bench marks of life, plunge him into the unknown, and he is shaken to the core. Like the Hebrew people in the unmarked wastes of the Sinai desert, he longs for the fleshpots and bondage of more familiar surroundings. He is a latter-day Moses who stands before the burning bush and yet demands that every contingency be accounted for before he ventures into the unknown.[40] He is a Solomon incapable of traveling within his own domain without the familiar sight of buildings and shrines that perpetuate his name. Knowing no "ultimate security beyond all the securities and insecurities," he is driven to the "idolatrous pursuit of false securities and redemptions." [41]

Tack It Down!

Whether manipulating the world or fleeing from it, the man of little faith seeks "something certain to cling to." Amid the uncertainties of earthly life he feels a need to have "something finished and complete." He erects a "narrow castle of certitude," an accomplishment, a virtue, a truth, "anything concrete." [42] For example, it may be a "security built on objectifying knowledge." Desiring the "safety of words and concepts," he involves himself in the "creation of certitude in systems of meaning": a doctrine, a principle, or a belief, preferably one claiming "eternal structures" or "some absoluteness." [43]

Behind every attempt to effect such "premature completions of life" lies a desire to "re-establish some sort of immediacy." In the face of the unknown he needs to "hold on to a support" and to orient himself by means of a "standpoint." [44] Simply put, he is the man who is unable to leave home without taking the furniture with him.

The Difference: Secure or Insecure in the Unknown?

Hence between the mature Christian person and his opposite lies a major difference. The mature Christian is able to "plunge himself into the life of a godless world without . . . trying to transfigure it." He "remains unshaken" on "unknown ground." [45] He can trust when trust is warranted. He trusts the foundations of existence, he trusts others, and he trusts himself. He harbors no deep-seated fears of life as it is in all its uncertainty and ambiguity. His sense of security rests on a broad experience of trusting relationships and can be shattered only by the erosion of these foundations. Thus he has learned to take things as they come and to welcome new experiences. The man lacking a mature Christian faith "cannot stand a world without God, whatever this God may be." [46] He is unable to trust. As an infant or an adult, he thinks, feels, and acts like a frightened child. He may express this more or less openly or attempt some strategy to overcome it. But every such strategy bears the indelible mark of a life-or-death struggle to maintain the familiar, and by this mark he can be known.

III

Helpful Aids to Surer Identification

Why We Need Something More

Often it is not enough simply to know what a mature Christian should look like. To have in mind the contrasting pictures of human characteristics sketched in the previous pages will undoubtedly help in indentifying certain persons or groups. A sensitive observer may require little more. But most of us have difficulty translating words and concepts, however concrete, into actual human feelings and behavior. This is especially true when we are considering persons who fall between the extremes described above. It may be that our powers of observation are not sufficiently developed or that we have a limited opportunity for observing. Yet even with the ability to make the most accurate on-the-spot observations of others, gross errors can still be made in weighing all relevant observations over a given period of time. Few of us have the right to trust our powers of observation and judgment this much.

Help Already at Hand

Indicators of nearly every characteristic of mature Christian life described above have been reported during the past twenty years in journals and books devoted to the study of personality and social psychology. These indicators run the gamut from the simplest paper-and-pencil tests to the most sophisticated experimental situations. Few, if any, were specifically designed to measure "Christian" characteristics; their intent is rather to more accurately identify people having certain characteristics of psychological interest. But when, almost despite themselves, these "empirical" indicators suggest central theological themes like those already discussed, they deserve further examination. Some prove unworthy of their promise. Either they do not validly reflect the intended theological meaning, or they are technically unreliable. Others withstand such critical appraisal, or at least incorporate features of particular value for more clearly identifying mature Christians. While even these instruments prove less accurate than we might hope, in most cases they are a considerable improvement over informal observation.

A Simple Sense-of-Security Test

Perhaps the most straightforward approach is found in the instrument that asks for a report of actual feelings and behavior. For example, the Ainsworth Security-Insecurity Tests[47] purport to measure a person's sense of basic security within the family (sample item: "Although I value the affection my parents hold for me, I feel that I do not need it to make me feel confident in myself"), in social life (sample item: "It makes me feel very uncomfortable to feel that someone dislikes me"), avocationally (sample item: "I am inclined to feel restless in my spare time"), and philosophically (sample item: "It makes me happy to feel that I have a worthwhile place in the world"). With over 150 such items, naturally some reflect the specific theological concerns of this chapter more than others. But if the respondent can be trusted to indicate how he feels on items of this type, these tests can be valuable indicators of security characteristics.

An even better instrument might be constructed by copying out a hundred or so descriptive statements from section II of this chapter and asking the respondent to indicate on the basis of a five-point scale how well each describes him. An even simpler form would be a list of adjectives[48] taken from a similar description of characteristics of the mature Christian life. The respondent would check only those he feels are "like me." [49]

How Well Can He Tolerate the Uncertain?

A number of instruments purporting to measure tolerance of ambiguity have also been developed. Budner[50] constructed a list of sixteen items incorporating three types of ambiguity: novelty, complexity, and insolubility. Respondents indicate on a six-point scale their agreement or disagreement with statements such as, "I would like to live in a foreign country for awhile" (novelty), "A good job is one where what is to be done and how it is to be done are always clear" (complexity), and "Many of our most important decisions are based upon insufficient information" (insolubility).[51] Items like these are usually answered honestly since few people feel flattered or embarrassed to admit their views on such seemingly "neutral" items.

The Simplest May Be the Soundest

Aside from their simplicity, the principal advantage of such paper-and-pencil self-report instruments is that they utilize the perception, experience, and judgment of the respondent. This is crucial where one's basic sense of security must be tapped. In a single item the respondent may be asked to review a lifetime of thought, feeling, and behavior, to sift relevant experiences, and to bring into play his powers of judgment. For the specific task at hand, no other type of instrument can tap so much relevant information.

The Value of Projective Tests

Projective tests provide a different type of advantage. A projective is by definition an ambiguous stimulus presented to the subject in order to observe the nature of his response. Types of stimuli may vary from simple visual, auditory, or tactile experiences to more complex social experiences. To the degree that ambiguity itself is perceived as threatening by insecure individuals, we should expect a response of anxiety, an attempt to structure the situation, or both. The content of the response may also prove revealing. Most projectives not only provide the stimulus, but also a number of indexes for identifying types of response.

The most widely used projective tests, the Rorschach and the Thematic Apperception Test (TAT), can be extremely helpful. However, interpretation and scoring require more skill and experience than can be easily acquired by the layman. Simpler projectives have been reported that suggest principles for equally imaginative test development. For example, Siegal [52] devised a test from sixteen pictures selected at random from a popular magazine. Each picture showed the head of an adult (not a public figure). Subjects were also given sixteen quotations clipped from magazines and told to match the statements with the pictures "if you feel any of the persons pictured made one of the statements." If not, they were to "leave the box blank." The subject who feels the need to find a quotation for most pictures is deemed to be inappropriately structuring.

A particularly intriguing type of projective finding wide use in the identification of security characteristics is one in which testing conditions and instructions are made highly ambiguous. Kenny and Ginsberg [53] gave subjects a number of wooden blocks of assorted sizes and colors with the instructions: "I would like you to figure out what is to be done with these and then go ahead and do it." The number of questions asked within a three-minute period was the only score, a higher number purporting to indicate greater intolerence of ambiguity and feelings of insecurity. The rationale is that, given such pronounced ambiguity, questions would be the most natural way to structure the situation.

Trust and Be Trustworthy

Finally, there are projective-type tests that indicate a person's ability to trust others. Bossom and Maslow [54] flashed two hundred yearbook photos on a screen to be judged either "warm" or "cold." The authors assume, and present evidence to suggest, that when confronted with ambiguous social stimuli (unfamiliar faces), a person tends to invest them with his general attitude or feelings toward others. An equally interesting design is in the form of a game.[55] Players may cooperate with each other to earn smaller amounts of money or compete against one another in hopes of winning larger amounts. Since the player who moves first is at the mercy of his partner, he makes either a "trusting" or "untrusting" move. His partner may then reciprocate with either a "trustworthy" or "untrustworthy" move. The author claims that both the ambiguity and the involvement of the game cause the players to reveal their basic dispositions to trust and to be trustworthy.

The Theology of the "Stressful Situation" Type Test

One of the most promising areas of personality measurement bearing upon Christian maturity has to do with the simulation of stressful situations. The theologically aware reader with an eye for experimental design is often impressed with the way the so-called "secular" discipline of personality study seems to catch the flavor of man's religious situation: the world as a source of threat, with possible responses of either fear (despair, delusion, pride, "works," etc.) or a deepening sense of security based upon trusting relationships. One is often struck by what seems to be the "demonic" ingenuity with which these designs seek out and threaten the Achilles' heel of each person's system of security, leaving him either to stand by a greater strength than that which has been experimentally weakened or to collapse with it.

A few general types of stress manipulations might be mentioned as illustrations. The most common, perhaps, is the induced failure situation. In this design the subject is given an ability test purported to be a reliable indicator of a culturally prized value, usually academic or vocational success. Some variations of the design call for an extremely difficult task at which the subject genuinely fails. Other variations allow the subject to complete the task but lead him to believe that he has performed very poorly. A third variation substitutes social rejection for task failure. Here the subject is made to believe that a peer group of a few hours' acquaintance does not value his presence.

Interpret the Parable

Regardless of how the situation is engineered, the purpose is to simulate the kind of stress found in real life and then observe what happens. For example, in separate experiments Dittes caused some (but not other) subjects to believe that they were socially rejected [56] or had failed a revealing aptitude test.[57] He then presented all subjects with a biblical "parable" from a recently discovered scroll, asking them to write their opinions concerning its meaning. The passage was in fact a series of garbled biblical symbols and idioms randomly juxtaposed by the experimenter and having no intelligible relation. The results showed that those led to feel unaccepted by their group or not likely to succeed in graduate school made significantly more attempts to impose a coherent meaning upon the passage than did those who were not threatened. Yet there were some in the threatened group who showed little need to impose structure where none existed.

Plunged into Darkness or Strange Worlds

Another type of stress manipulation involves darkness. The subject plunged into darkness in unfamiliar surroundings has little outside himself to cling to for support. The auto-kinetic effect provides an example of how people react to this situation. In the autokinetic effect a stationary point of light in a darkened room appears to move. The experience is common to most persons. What is uncommon is the character of the apparent movement. Millon[58] asked his subjects to report both the distance and direction of light movement. Trials were continued until a criterion of ten out of thirteen similar reports were given by each subject. Those who were found by independent measurement least able to tolerate ambiguity established response patterns five times as quickly as their more tolerant counterparts. Taft [59] found that subjects reporting significantly less light movement tended also to be those with higher intolerance of ambiguity. These findings generally support the theory that the insecure person under stress will involuntarily "hold on" to the familiar, while his freer counterpart will allow himself to experience the new and the strange.

The flicker fusion test presents a different kind of visual illusion in darkness. As reported by Gardner,[60] three cards are projected on a screen successively from left to right. On the first and third cards a figure of a horse is printed, the middle card being blank. At the lowest projection speeds the subject sees two horses flashing on and off on alternate sides of the screen. As the speed is increased, the subject suddenly sees a single horse moving back and forth across the screen. As the speed is further increased, there is another point at which the subject becomes aware that the two horses are flashing on and off simultaneously as two separate entities. The distance (in cycles per second) between the onset of these last two reported visual experiences is scored. Of the three visual illusions the most realistic and familiar are the initial and final state during which the two horses are seen in their "proper" places on opposite sides of the screen. The subject whose feelings of security require that things appear as they are "known to be" will see the horse move back and forth across the screen only briefly, while the more stable individual will tolerate this inconsistency and experience the movement significantly longer.[61]

Tolerance for unrealistic experiences is also the basis for a number of studies using aniseikonic lenses. The lenses stimulate a visual aberration called aniseikonia that causes things to appear a different size and shape. The experience of distortion is not immediate, but develops gradually. There is usually less distortion of familiar objects than of unfamiliar. Nevertheless, it has been found that people vary considerably with respect to both the speed and extent of distortion. A number of investigators[62] have shown that persons who most resist the progress of this bizarre experience are those who tend to structure experience in other areas of their lives.

Simulating the Jobian Prologue

In general it is the ability to deal with the incongruous, the unfamiliar, and other threatening aspects of life without clinging to or creating false securities that distinguishes the man of faith from the idolater in Christian thought. The experimenter attempts to simulate these stressful life situations and invents often ingenious ways to observe the results. He demonstrates that as the safe and familiar aspects of life are diminished, a certain type of individual seeks to compensate for this loss by an increase in restructuring activity through fantasy or environmental manipulation. To the degree that the attempt to restructure can be experimentally frustrated, this type of individual may also experience genuine terror and anxiety.

The individual whose attitude and activities do not evidence a struggle to maintain the familiar lies at the opposite end of the experimenter's bell curve. Like Kierkegaard's "knight of faith," outwardly he may resemble his less secure brother. But to one able to "experimentally observe" critical feelings and varying behaviors under certain conditions, the difference is like that between night and day.[63]

A Good Start—But Not Enough

Were tests and measures like those described in section III of this chapter truly adequate indicators of those characteristics portrayed in section II, there would be little need for continuing. In time we may have such instruments, but we do not have them now. To increase the accuracy with which persons can be distinguished at present, we will focus upon four specific abilities central to the functioning of the mature Christian: self-knowledge, honest expression, accurate perception, and adequate response. In the following four chapters each will be presented in "clinical" fashion with sample theological sources and empirical indicators, as in this chapter.

Generally speaking, we can understand the impairment of these four constituent abilities in precisely the same terms as we have been using to understand the man of little faith. Each type of impairment is a means of escape, a learned response to a deep-seated fear of ambiguity and its conditioned correlate, terror.

To be specific, the two perceptual distortions, one a distortion of the self (Chaper III) and the other of the world (Chapter V), should be favored by those who have learned to escape by means of fantasy, delusion, or distorted perception. The two response restrictions, one a restriction of response to inner events (Chapter IV) and the other to outer events (Chapter VI), are more likely to be favored by those who have sought to escape by manipulative techniques, i.e., controlling themselves or controlling others to gain acceptance. Only the openly fearful, depressed, or anxious person will receive no further attention in this volume since he is easily identified either by observation or by any reliable security-insecurity test.

IV

How to Proceed from Here

The four chapters to follow are on the same pattern as this and may be read in any order desired. Each adds another piece to the picture. Now that you have a feel for what is to come, put yourself (and the book) to the test. Pick out someone you know and keep him—or *her* if you can transpose —in mind while reading the next chapter. Granting that he will fit neither the ideal type nor the anti-type described where would you place him on a continuum between the two?

If you need help, look up a few of the footnoted theological references at the end of the chapter. They will provide a broader context for understanding the area you may be having trouble with. Likewise, don't neglect the empirical studies. Often just understanding how an experimental situation works can sharpen your eye for life situations embodying the same "operational definitions" of behavior. The journal articles reporting these are typically only a few pages and, like the theological contexts, help clarify the fit between what you see on the page and what you see in a human being.

NOTES

1. John Calvin, *Institutes of the Christian Religion*, Vols. I and II, trans. Henry Beveridge (Grand Rapids: Eerdmans, 1962), Bk. iii, chap. 2, sec. 7 (hereafter cited as iii.2, 7).

2. H. Richard Niebuhr, *The Purpose of the Church and Its Ministry*, in collaboration with Daniel Day Williams and James M. Gustafson (New York: Harper, 1956), p. 37.

3. Calvin, *Institutes*, iii.2., 16; Friedrich Schleiermacher, *The Christian Faith*, ed. H. R. Mackintosh and J. S. Stewart (Edinburgh: T. & T. Clark, 1928), p. 11; cf. Karl Barth, *Church Dogmatics*, IV/2, ed. G. W. Bromiley and T. F. Torrance, trans. G. W. Bromiley (Edinburgh: T. & T. Clark, 1958), 728-29.

4. Karl Barth, *Church Dogmatics*, IV/1, ed. G. W. Bromiley and T. F. Torrance, trans. G. W. Bromiley (Edinburgh: T. & T. Clark, 1956), 748, cf. pp. 766, 769; Martin Luther, *Lectures on Galatians 1535, Chapters 1-4*, ed. and trans. Jaroslav Pelikan ("Luther's Works," Vol. XXVI; St. Louis: Concordia, 1963), pp. 42, 179; Calvin, *Institutes*, iii.24, 7; Schleiermacher, *Christian Faith*, p. 68.

5. H. Richard Niebuhr, *The Responsible Self* (New York: Harper, 1963), p. 177; Luther, *Galatians 1-4*, pp. 4-5; Paul Tillich, *The Shaking of the Foundations* (New York: Scribner's, 1948), p. 59; cf. Calvin, *Institutes*, iii.2, 7; Barth, IV/1, 775.

6. Søren Kierkegaard, *Fear and Trembling and the Sickness unto Death*, trans. Walter Lowrie (Garden City, N. Y.: Doubleday, 1954), p. 51; Rudolf Bultmann, *et al.*, *Kerygma and Myth: A Theological Debate*, ed. Hans. W. Bartsch (New York: Harper, 1961), p. 203; Barth, IV/1, 769; IV/2, 536-37; cf. IV/1, 775; Calvin, *Institutes*, i.17, 9; iii.2, 21; Schleiermacher, *Christian Faith*, p. 433; Karl Barth, *Church Dogmatics*, IV/3(2), ed. G. W. Bromiley and T. F. Torrance, trans. G. W. Bromiley (Edinburgh: T. & T. Clark, 1962), 645; Reinhold Niebuhr, *The Nature and Destiny of Man* (New York: Scribner's, 1964), 320-21.

7. Paul Tillich, *The Courage to Be* (New Haven: Yale University Press, 1952), p. 86; Calvin, *Institutes*, iii.19, 5; Rudolf Bultmann, *Essays: Philosophical and Theological*, trans. James C. G. Greig (New York: Macmillan, 1955), p. 6; Luther, *Galatians 1-4*, p. 379.

8. Tillich, *Shaking of the Foundations*, p. 162.

9. Bultmann, *Essays*, p. 167, cf. pp. 45-46; Paul Tillich, *Systematic Theology*, III (Chicago: University of Chicago Press, 1963), 234; *Dynamics of Faith* (New York: Harper, 1957), p. 20; Dietrich Bonhoeffer, *Life Together*, trans. John W. Doberstein (New York: Harper, 1954), p. 96; Søren Kierkegaard, *Training in Christianity and the Edifying Discourse Which Accompanied It*, trans. Walter Lowrie (London: Oxford University Press, 1941), pp. 55, 80; Rudolf Bultmann, *Existence and Faith: Shorter Writings of Rudolf Bultmann*, trans. Shubert M. Ogden (Meridian Books; Cleveland: World, 1960), pp. 260-61; Luther, *Galatians 1-4*, p. 99.

10. Bonhoeffer, *Life Together*, pp. 106-9; John Calvin, *Calvin: Commentaries*, trans. Joseph Haroutunian and Louise P. Smith ("Library of

Christian Classics," Vol. XXIII; Philadelphia: Westminster, 1958), p. 321; Bultmann, *Essays*, pp. 294-96; Karl Barth, *Church Dogmatics*, III/2, ed. G. W. Bromiley and T. F. Torrance, trans. Harold Knight, *et al.* (Edinburgh: T. & T. Clark, 1960), 254; Martin Luther, *Lectures on Romans*, trans. Wilhelm Pauck ("Library of Christian Classics," Vol. XV; Philadelphia: Westminster, 1961), p. 103; Dietrich Bonhoeffer, *Letters and Papers from Prison*, ed. Eberhard Bethge, trans. R. H. Fuller (New York: Macmillan, 1953), pp. 105, 219.

11. Reinhold Niebuhr, *An Interpretation of Christian Ethics* (Meridian Books; Cleveland: World, 1956), p. 85.

12. Kierkegaard, *Fear and Trembling*, pp. 49-51; H. Richard Niebuhr, *The Meaning of Revelation* (New York: Macmillan, 1960), p. 114; Martin Luther, "Two Kinds of Righteousness," trans. Lowell J. Satre, *Career of the Reformer: I*, ed. Harold J. Grimm ("Luther's Works," Vol. XXXI; Philadelphia: Muhlenberg, 1957), pp. 302-3; Bonhoeffer, *Life Together*, p. 88; *Letters and Papers*, pp. 222-23.

13. Søren Kierkegaard, *Concluding Unscientific Postscript to the Philosophical Fragments*, trans. David F. Swenson (Princeton: Princeton University Press, 1941), p. 180; Bonhoeffer, *Letters and Papers*, p. 28; cf. Bultmann, *Essays*, p. 175; *Kerygma and Myth*, p. 33; Barth, IV/1, 775.

14. Tillich, *Shaking of the Foundations*, p. 59; Rudolf Bultmann, *Jesus Christ and Mythology* (New York: Scribner's, 1958), p. 31; cf. Dietrich Bonhoeffer, *The Cost of Discipleship*, trans. R. H. Fuller (New York: Macmillan, 1959), pp. 62-63; H. Richard Niebuhr, *Responsible Self*, pp. 118-19; *Purpose of the Church*, p. 37.

15. Luther, *Galatians 1-4*, p. 99; cf. Calvin, *Institutes*, ii.15, 4; Barth, IV/2, 541; IV/3(2); 654; *Church Dogmatics*, IV/3(1), ed. G. W. Bromiley and T. F. Torrance, trans. G. W. Bromiley (Edinburgh: T. &. T. Clark, 1961), p. 448; Bonhoeffer, *Letters and Papers*, p. 201.

16. H. Richard Niebuhr, *Responsible Self*, p. 177; Kierkegaard, *Training in Christianity*, p. 55; Barth, IV/3(2), 928; cf. Kierkegaard, *Fear and Trembling*, pp. 49-51; *Postscript*, pp. 440-41; *Training in Christianity*, p. 71; Bonhoeffer, *Cost of Discipleship*, p. 199; Friedrich Schleiermacher, *On Religion: Speeches to Its Cultured Despisers*, trans. John Oman (New York: Harper, 1958), p. 12.

17. Heb. 11:8-9.

18. Gen. 12:1, 4a.

19. Bonhoeffer, *Cost of Discipleship*, p. 103.

20. Martin Luther, "A Mighty Fortress Is Our God."

21. Tillich, *Shaking of the Foundations*, p. 170; *Dynamics of Faith*, pp. 19-20; Bultmann, *Essays*, p. 53; cf. Martin Luther, *Lectures on Galatians 1535, Chapters 5-6*, *Lectures on Galatians 1519, Chapters 1-6*, ed. and trans. Jaroslav Pelikan ("Luther's Works," Vol. XXVII; St. Louis: Concordia, 1964), p. 13; Bultmann, *Existence and Faith*, p. 218; Reinhold Niebuhr, *Nature and Destiny of Man*, I, 27; Bonhoeffer, *Life Together*, p. 76; Barth, IV/3(1), 672-73.

22. Bultmann, *Christ and Mythology*, p. 41; Tillich, *Dynamics of Faith*, p. 19; Barth, IV/3(1), 672-73; cf. Kierkegaard, *Postscript*, p. 43; Bonhoeffer, *Life Together*, p. 88.

23. Tillich, *Courage to Be*, pp. 49-50, *Shaking of the Foundations*, p. 97;

Bultmann, *Essays*, p. 6; cf. Bultmann, *Existence and Faith*, p. 218; Barth, IV/2, 460-63; Schleiermacher, *On Religion*, p. 12; Tillich, *Courage to Be*, p. 38; Kierkegaard, *Postscript*, p. 485; Barth, IV/2, 93; H. Richard Niebuhr, *Responsible Self*, pp. 67, 116, 118.

24. Gen. 11:4; Mark 9:5; Luke 12:13-14.

25. Schleiermacher, *On Religion*, p. 20; Bonhoeffer, *Cost of Discipleship*, p. 63; cf. Kierkegaard, *Postscript*, pp. 43, 79; Bultmann, *Essays*, pp. 174-75; Bonhoeffer, *Life Together*, pp. 108-9; Tillich, *Courage to Be*, p. 189; Barth, IV/3(1), 448.

26. II Sam. 11.

27. Dietrich Bonhoeffer, *Ethics*, ed. Eberhard Bethge, trans. Neville H. Smith (New York: Macmillan, 1955) p. 237; cf. Calvin, *Institutes*, iv.10, 10, and ii.3, 3; Kierkegaard, *Training in Christianity*, p. 236; *Postscript*, pp. 121, 206-7; Tillich, *Shaking of the Foundations*, pp. 97, 170; *Courage to Be*, pp. 49-50; *Systematic Theology*, III, 103; Luther, *Galatians 1-4*, pp. 404, 430-31.

28. Bonhoeffer, *Life Together*, pp. 108-9; cf. Karl Barth, *Church Dogmatics*, III/4, ed. G. W. Bromiley and T. F. Torrance, trans. A. T. Mackay, *et al.* (Edinburgh: T. & T. Clark, 1961), 673; Kierkegaard, *Postscript*, p. 452; *Training in Christianity*, p. 268; Søren Kierkegaard, *For Self-examination*, trans. Edna Hong and Howard Hong (Minneapolis: Augsburg, 1940), p. 27.

29. Barth, IV/2, 473; Bonhoeffer, *Ethics*, p. 164; Reinhold Niebuhr, *Nature*, pp. 191-92.

30. Kierkegaard, *Postscript*, pp. 121, 321; Barth, IV/2, 668; cf. Bonhoeffer, *Ethics*, p. 237.

31. Luther, *Galatians 1-4*, pp. 8-9; *Galatians 5-6*, pp. 8, 13; cf. Reinhold Niebuhr, *Nature*, p. 272; Calvin, *Commentaries*, p. 224; Tillich, *Systematic Theology*, III, 232-33; Reinhold Niebuhr, *Interpretation*, p. 48; Bultmann, *Essays*, p. 60.

32. Schleiermacher, *On Religion*, p. 20; Tillich, *Dynamics of Faith*, p.104; *Courage to Be*, p. 69; cf. Søren Kierkegaard, *Works of Love*, trans. David F. and Lillian M. Swenson (Princeton: Princeton University Press, 1946), p. 130; Bultmann, *Essays*, p. 8; *Kerygma and Myth*, p. 19; Bonhoeffer, *Life Together*, p. 27.

33. Reinhold Niebuhr, *Nature*, pp. 137-38; *Destiny*, p. 63.

34. Kierkegaard, *Postscript*, p. 308; cf. Kierkegaard, *Fear and Trembling*, pp. 49-51; Bultmann, *Essays*, pp. 147-48; Tillich, *Dynamics of Faith*, p. 101; *Courage to Be*, pp. 49-50, *Shaking of the Foundations*, p. 170.

35. Schleiermacher, *Christian Faith*, p. 13; cf. Kierkegaard, *Postscript*, pp. 308, 317; Bonhoeffer, *Ethics*, p. 250; *Letters and Papers*, p. 125.

36. Barth, III/2, 251; IV/2, 745; cf. Bultmann, *Existence and Faith*, pp. 214, 218; Schleiermacher, *Christian Faith*, pp. 432-33, 726-27; Barth, III/2, 226-27, 246; Reinhold Niebuhr, *Destiny*, pp. 94-95.

37. Bonhoeffer, *Life Together*, pp. 27, 76; cf. Calvin, *Institutes*, ii.2, 15.

38. Barth, IV/2, 745; Bultmann, *Essays*, pp. 8, 40; cf. Bultmann, *Essays*, pp. 294, 295, 300-301; Barth, III/2, 254; Bonhoeffer, *Life Together*, pp. 112-13.

39. Bonhoeffer, *Ethics*, pp. 197-98.

40. Exod. 16:2-3; 3:1–4:17.

41. Reinhold Niebuhr, *Destiny*, pp. 320-21.
42. Kierkegaard, *Postscript*, pp. 43, 79; Tillich, *Courage to Be*, pp. 76, 189.
43. Bultmann, *Christ and Mythology*, p. 84; Tillich, *Courage to Be*, p. 76; Paul Tillich, *The Protestant Era*, trans. James L. Adams (abridged ed; Chicago: University of Chicago Press, 1957), p. 215.
44. Reinhold Niebuhr, *Destiny*, p. 125; Bonhoeffer, *Life Together*, pp. 108-9; Bultmann, *Essays*, pp. 174-75.
45. Bonhoeffer, *Letters and Papers*, pp. 222-23; Tillich, *Shaking of the Foundations*, p. 59.
46. Tillich, *Courage to Be*, pp. 182-83.
47. Leonard H. Ainsworth and Mary D. Ainsworth, *Measuring Security in Personal Adjustment* (Toronto: University of Toronto Press, 1958), pp. 89-95.
48. C. L. Bruninga, *et al.*, "Some Effects of Pastoral Visitation with Mental Patients" (Norwich, Conn.: Norwich State Hospital, 1967).
49. A certain caution must be exercised with all homemade instruments to insure adequate reliability and to neutralize built-in biases. Standard texts such as Lee Cronback, *Essentials of Psychological Testing* (New York: Harper, 1969), will aid substantially in cultivating an awareness of these factors.
50. Stanley Budner, "Intolerance of Ambiguity as a Personality Variable," *Journal of Personality*, XXX (1962), 29-50.
51. This is an exceptional instrument because of the care with which social desirability, acquiescence, and other possible artifacts have been neutralized. Seventeen samples averaging forty subjects apiece were used to develop the instrument. Test-retest reliability (two weeks to two months) was .85 for a tested sample. While essentially construct validated, it has correlated .36 to .54 with three other intolerance of ambiguity instruments.
52. Sidney Siegal, "Certain Determinants and Correlates of Authoritarianism," *Genetic Psychology Monographs*, XLIX (1954), 187-229.
53. Douglas T. Kenny and Rose Ginsberg, "The Specificity of Intolerance of Ambiguity Measures," *Journal of Abnormal and Social Psychology*, LVI (1958), 300-305.
54. Joseph Bossom and A. H. Maslow, "Security of Judges as a Factor in Impressions of Warmth in Others," *Journal of Abnormal and Social Psychology*, LV (1957), 147-48.
55. Morton Deutsch, "Trust, Trustworthiness, and the F-Scale," *Journal of Abnormal and Social Psychology*, LXI (1960), 138-40.
56. James E. Dittes, "Effect of Changes in Self-esteem upon Impulsiveness and Deliberation in Making Judgments," *Journal of Abnormal and Social Psychology*, LVIII (1959), 348-56.
57. James E. Dittes, "Impulsive Closure as Reaction to Failure-induced Threat," *Journal of Abnormal and Social Psychology*, LXIII (1961), 562-69.
58. Theodore Millon, "Authoritariansim, Intolerance of Ambiguity, and Rigidity Under Ego- and Task-involving Conditions," *Journal of Abnormal and Social Psychology*, LV (1957), 29-33.
59. Ronald Taft, "Intolerance of Ambiguity and Ethnocentrism," *Journal of Consulting Psychology*, XX (1956), 153-54.

60. Riley W. Gardner, *et al.*, "Cognitive Control: A Study of Individual Consistency in Cognitive Behavior," *Psychological Issues*, I (1959), 33-34.

61. George S. Klein and Herbert J. Schlesinger, " 'Perceptual Attitudes' Toward Instability: I. Prediction of Apparent Movement Experiences from Rorschach Responses," *Journal of Personality*, XIX (1951), 289-302.

62 Gardner, "Cognitive Control," pp. 33-34; Barclay Martin, "Intolerance of Ambiguity in Interpersonal and Perceptual Behavior," *Journal of Personality*, XXII (1954), 494-503; Joy M. Kaplan, "Predicting Memory Behavior from Cognitive Attitudes Toward Instability," *American Psychologist*, VII (1952), 322; Wesley C. Becker, "Perceptual Rigidity as Measured by Aniseikonic Lenses," *Journal of Abnormal and Social Psychology*, XLIX (1954), 419-22.

63. Kierkegaard, *Postscript*, pp. 446, 451, 540, 544.

---chapter III---

HE CAN SEE HIMSELF
AS HE REALLY IS

I

The Importance of Self-knowledge for the Christian Life

To be a Christian is to know oneself. While seldom stated
so directly, knowledge of the self has been presumed central
to the Christian life since the time of Jesus.

How It Developed

In the early centuries it was mainly the need for contrition that demanded ruthless self-appraisal. The first
step toward the Christian life was knowing the worst in
oneself. As long as a man continued to flatter himself and
cover up his faults, he remained imprisoned by the power
of sin. Once he was able to see himself clearly in the light
of the gospel, however, sin would begin to lose its hold.
The Christian-to-be could then pour out his sins in confession. When confessed, these secret thoughts and shameful

deeds could be forgiven. Forgiveness, in turn, was the condition of saving grace. By the undisputed laws of this primitive Christian psychology, the lofty goal of Christian life was seen to rest finally upon the bedrock of the self-knowledge.

The Protestant Reformation did little to alter the place or importance of self-knowledge in the economy of salvation. If anything, it quickened a sensitivity to the mortal dangers of self-deception. These dangers became a primary concern of the reformers because of their conviction that the medieval church had become a stumbling block to true self-knowledge and thus to contrition, confession, forgiveness, and saving faith.

Recent trends in Protestant thought show no less concern for inner honesty but do indicate a shifting emphasis in the role of self-knowledge. To the reformers, true knowledge of the self made possible saving faith by emptying the soul of false opinions and idolatrous affections. Although this was not accomplished without the power of grace, the emphasis was decidedly on its preparatory function: the old man must be put off before the new man could live. The direction of contemporary theology has been to reverse this emphasis. It has tended to regard self-knowledge as a fruit of grace, both as a sign of spiritual health and as a means for enabling an unjaundiced view of the world.

A Psychological Correlate

A result of this more complex view has been to nourish a theological interest in the insights and techniques of psychotherapy. It is hardly a coincidence that both growth in the Christian life and growth in emotional maturity begin at the point where a man is able to be honest with himself about himself. While some modern theologians can be justly censured for uncritically equating theological and psychological views of human nature, a sound psychological understanding of the ways of human self-deception immeasurably enriches theological understanding.

This is especially true where behavior is concerned. Why a man will deceive himself is often profoundly understood by traditional theology—but not the myriad ways in which he does it. Seemingly neutral behaviors assume theological significance when we grasp from whence they stem. For this reason the description to follow (especially where specific illustrations are given) is informed by what the clinically oriented psychologist has observed in those both able and unable to appraise themselves accurately. Descriptive essentials, of course, continue to be derived from Protestant thought.

II

The Person Who Knows Himself

In terms of simple description we speak of a person who "knows himself." It is not so much that he knows certain facts about himself, although this may be involved. Nor does this person often bring into awareness the full extent of his knowledge, since he is not particularly given to "introspection." [1] Rather, he is distinguished by his ability to see himself as he really is when the occasion demands, especially in those areas of his life that seem the most important to him. [2]

The Face in the Mirror

At the simplest level this means that he has a sane estimate of his gifts. [3] Does he enjoy good health or bad? He will be able to tell you. He can describe his physical appearance without overlooking plain or overprominent features, a slight stoop or an irregular gait, graying or receding hair, and similar legacies. His particular family, national, racial, or religious inheritance is known and acknowledged, whether he is proud of it or not. He remembers as much of what he has been told about his ancestors with the funny-sounding names as he does about the ones who debarked from the *Mayflower*.

What he knows of himself will be reflected as well in what he does with his endowments. As a youth he is not likely to incur a hernia the first week on a summer construction job or a pulled leg muscle during the first week of football practice. Advancing age will be appropriately acknowledged by less strenuous exertion on the tennis court or with the snow shovel. In a word, he has a "clearer and more sober estimate" of his own limitations. He sees his gifts objectively at the very point where objectivity is the most difficult.[4]

The same is true of his acquired skills, abilities, and characteristics. If he is academically inclined, he will neither overestimate nor underestimate his scholastic skills. He will "call them what they are."[5] He can "see himself" as a B+ student despite his aspirations for A's or a temporary run of C's. Whether or not he is a brilliant conversationalist, a graceful dancer, or a skillful mediator, he seldom confuses a desire for competence with the fact of accomplishment. "What he would like to have and to be" remains distinct from what he has and is.[6] After twenty years of TV repairing, insurance selling, teaching school, or taxi driving, he has a pretty fair idea of how good he is. At least he will picture his degree of competence largely the way his clients, colleagues, and competitors do.[7]

There is also a striking realism about the way such a person views his special interests and hobbies. He is aware of what he knows and does not know about home repair, foreign affairs, the Los Angeles Dodgers, and new cars. He also knows what kind of personality he shows the world. He will recognize a good character description of himself as readily as he will identify his own photograph and will know when he is being stuffy or boastful and when he is being likable and genuine.

At a Distance

Such knowledge would be impossible did he not have the "power of transcending" the situation in which he finds himself.[8] As husband and father, professional authority, or moral example, he knows the consequences of failure. Yet amid the pressing demands of life he "perceives the limitations" of his achievements as well as his own propensity to minimize them.[9] Catching these occasional glimpses of himself from beyond himself, he is able to see the humor in what he does, expecially in "senseless" attempts to take himself too seriously.[10] For example, when a double entendre brings peals of laughter in the midst of a heated discussion, he can both see and enjoy the humor of his unintended slip. That night he may share the joke with his wife or friends, especially if it brought to nought a subtle attempt to delude himself. He is the person who can laugh at his own acknowledged attempts at self-deception while realistically appraising his degree of success in resisting them.

For this reason he is able also to resist the temptation of prolonged "self-investigations." [11] He returns to himself in an instant to act on the basis of a more accurate conception of himself. Knowing better "what he has not and is not" on the basis of his past, he is also better able to appraise what he can and cannot do in the future.[12] Important changes in vocation or marriage rarely prove unwise. If he takes the time to dismantle his wife's broken sewing machine, he'll most likely succeed in fixing it. Yet when confronted by a task of limitless demands and responsibility, he may accept its challenge and risk without presuming limitless abilities. He will do what he can do and won't "torture himself" about what he cannot do—supposing somehow that he might have done it.[13] He knows what he can handle and what he can't.

Aware of His Feelings

The Christian life is also known by its sensitivity to the "knowledge of the really real in ourselves."[14] Although more is involved than what was once meant by being "conscious of the desires of the flesh,"[15] the classic desires of lust, anger, and pride are among the most difficult to acknowledge inwardly. The Christian feels the full strength of these desires; he may control them—or he may not—but he does not suppress them into forgetfulness.[16] When he is angry, he knows that he is angry and at whom. If he is angry at himself for losing a cuff link, he won't deliberately find fault with the breakfast coffee. If his boss crosses him on a matter of some importance, he is not likely to feel guilty about it himself or, with "illusions about the Turk," take it out on the office boy.[17] Frustration may stir feelings of irritation against those who would least understand them, yet he remains aware of his own unpleasantness.

The Christian is also aware of his sexual feelings. Whether young or old, married or single, he knows which persons and what things arouse him. An attractive woman or a sensuous novel may win his respect for many other qualities, but he is also aware of whatever erotic feelings they elicit. Nor is this awareness confined to garden-variety sexuality. As a father he is conscious of how his daughter may stimulate him. He can recognize a sexual attraction toward his mother and his father in his feeling of love for them, and he is as perceptive about these feelings toward others of his own sex. A good friend, a total stranger, a tight-jeaned teen-ager or a little child will not frighten him into an inward denial of sexual feelings they may arouse. Able to "lure forth the obscure libido," he is a man of many sexual feelings who can acknowledge them to himself.[18]

Feelings of apprehension are as easily recognized. He will not be tortured by unrealistic fears, but he may be knowingly concerned about a number of things: failing health, signs of a business recession, his daughter's dating habits, his son's draft status, etc. What he has done may cause him to feel guilty. What he must do may cause him some anxiety. Yet he can think of these things without disguising or deadening their pain.[19] By the same measure, whatever is experienced as pleasurable is not transformed in his mind into something less enjoyable. He "does not need to contort his good works into bad," or "consider frantically or artificially his immoralities." Good and bad feelings, like good and bad deeds, are seen for what they are.[20] He is, in fact, a person whose emotional awareness is governed more by how important a feeling is to him than by what *kind* of importance it has for him.

"In My Members Another Law"

Nor does he see himself feeling merely one thing or another. He is also aware of "ambiguities in himself" and of conflicting emotions.[21] At times he senses himself going in two directions at once, "aware of a split in himself" and of being torn apart by seemingly contrary desires.[22] He may sense, for example, that he views a forthcoming promotion with both joy and dread or an impending operation with both hope and fear. He can be aware of entertaining a secret wish for a friend's misfortune at the instant he whole-heartedly desires his success. An impending riot may awaken a desire for rebellion as well as a fear that things will get out of hand. All this he senses, even though doing so requires that he understand himself as existing in the "greatest oppositions." [23] He knows himself as a person who craves both dependence and independence, who desires to do evil as well as good, and who both loves and is angry with those closest to him. It may very well be that he wonders why he feels this way. He may be dismayed that he feels this way. But his awareness of what he feels is remarkably accurate.

Memories—Pleasant and Painful

What he remembers about himself is no less important. He has, in fact, a better-than-average memory for most personally exciting and upsetting experiences, even when similar feelings accompany their recall. "He does not 'forget' in the least what lies behind him." [24] The shame of being caught at stealing as a child, the distressing experience of maintaining a lie before his parents, sexual misadventures in adolescence, and the feeling of having hurt someone deeply—these, no less than the happier memories of his successes and kindnesses, take their rightful place in his conception of himself. Through his past he has a "profound insight into his own inmost heart." [25] He knows his weaknesses and his propensity to yield to temptations, especially the more subtle ones. Yet he is equally aware of where he has succeeded in overcoming these.[26] He lives with the knowledge that he is both normal and abnormal, virtuous and lacking virtue, always succeeding and yet always failing. Like the father of the epileptic boy brought before Jesus, he is able to see both his strength and his weakness at the very moment that such knowledge might prove to be the undoing of all that he desires.[27]

The Life of Self-deception

There is also the kind of person who knows less about himself than do his friends. He confuses reality with wish, believing himself to be what he would like to be or what he perceives his friends want him to be.[28] Because he is unable to make a realistic separation between fact and fantasy, his actions are often tinged with irony.[29] In the evening he sits at the table with his best friend and says, "If I must die with you, I will not deny you." A few hours later he denies him three times, and without apparent awareness of the inconsistency.[30] Or when confronted with an accurate but unflattering picture of himself, he will say with Saul, "I have done wrong; . . . behold, I have played the fool, and have erred exceedingly," and then act in complete disregard of this knowledge.[31]

Out of Touch with Himself

Not only do such a person's words contradict his actions, but they bear little relation to his inner world. What he knows of himself and describes as himself remains insulated from his world of feelings, desires, and emotions. "Even trifling self-revelations" are met with a "tremendous force of resistance." [32] He may inwardly feel inferior to others but believe himself to be superior. Seldom will he see the depth of his mistrust toward his friends, the jealously he has for a colleague, or his envy of a competitor. He is often blind to his fear of another's intentions toward him and oftener still cannot recognize the fear that he has of his own desires. Like the elder brother in the parable of the Prodigal Son, he may protest his fidelity, unaware of the smoldering resentment he has harbored for his father.[33] So little does he know of his own feelings that he either "does not even notice" them or he attributes them to others.[34]

This is particularly evident in the sexual area. He may be sexually attracted to a woman yet "in the dark about his own motives."[35] If he is inclined toward moralism, he may dedicate himself to previewing smutty films and publications in order to protect others from their perverse influence. If he considers himself liberal in sexual matters, he may have considerable difficulty recognizing his own fears of sexual inadequacy. Nor will he be aware of his feminine traits and sentiments. Whatever his sexual views, it is unlikely that he knows the extent to which common homosexual desires and fears dictate his choice of actual or fantasied women. That which he believes to be love for another may be little more than reflected self-love. In fact, nearly everything commonly meant by "sexuality" will dramatically illustrate his propensity for self-deception.

The Partial Past

Finally, there is the matter of forgetting. Such a person is often able to "hold a good opinion of himself" because he has simply forgotten the relevant facts of his life on which a less flattering opinion might be based.[36] He has an uncanny memory for things he has done well and a curious amnesia for his failures. It is his hits and not the strikeouts, or the tackles that he made and not those he missed, that most readily come to mind when he reflects on the sandlot activities of his youth. From his student days he remembers more of the A's and B's than the C's and D's he received. Failure is forgotten more often than accomplishment, especially when it touches a prided ability. For instance, he is more likely to remember the leaky pipe that he fixed than the one he finally had to get the plumber for. Try as he might, what can be recalled of the past will be biased in favor of his more admired achievements.

Moral and ethical issues will certainly illustrate this tendency. It is probable that such a person will have a clearer recall for having been treated unfairly than for having treated others unfairly. Similarly, his virtues will outshine his selfishness. He will "flatter" his conscience and "most willingly persuade" himself of his righteousness.[37] Kindness for kindness, dollar for dollar, what he has given will outweigh in his mind what he has received. Unlike the publican who beat his breast at the painful remembrance of his sins, he resembles the Pharisee who stood before God in virtual ignorance of his sins, remembering only what was safe to remember.[38] So greatly does this person fear a chance meeting with his true self that he ingeniously cloaks his life with a mantle of fantasy. He "hides his nothingness from himself" because "he cannot bear the sight of it." [39] Shameful deeds of the past dissolve before his eyes until he no longer is able to recognize himself. He is like David, who mentally so insulated himself from his dealings with Bathsheba and her husband that he failed to see himself in Nathan's parable.[40]

Thus whatever is of greatest importance in his life, whether achievement, virtue, or social acclaim, he seeks to embody it by erasing from his mind every part of himself which threatens its plausibility. Inwardly desiring to "deceive himself about himself," [41] he may come to know who he is perhaps only on those rare occasions when some Nathan has the temerity to strip away the mask and announce: "You are the man." [42]

The Crucial Difference

Hence the life touched with Christian freedom and grace can be distinguished from the life that is not by the degree to which a person is "clear" about himself at those points which most deeply affect his feelings of security.[43] The

Christian senses that his life does not depend upon what he thinks of himself. He is therefore free to know both the best and the worst in himself. He "pretends" nothing, "conceals" nothing, and "remembers everything" that bears importantly upon his life.[44] The person untouched by grace lacks a sense of security apart from successful self-deception. He willingly persuades himself of a false righteousness. What begins in fearful denial soon becomes "unconscious ignorance" until little of the true self can be recognized except that which happens to "fit in with the picture of the self we cherish." [45] As for the rest, he will "push it down into the sub-conscious" to avoid confronting the truth about himself.[46]

III

Indicators of Self-knowledge

Why Here?

Despite the fact that we are now dealing with a behavioral characteristic far more restricted in scope than the one considered in the preceding chapter, a characteristic more obviously an ability possessed or not possessed than a global feeling or disposition, there is still a need for empirical indicators of self-knowledge.

Few persons known to us display either the extreme insight or self-deception described above. Most people fit somewhere between. Nevertheless, we would like to be able to tell how much insight or self-deception characterizes their style of life. With these persons we are probably no closer to knowing a mature Christian for merely having described the parameters of self-knowledge. Armed only with a mental picture of opposite types, the average untrained observer will have difficulty with most attempted identifications not obviously bordering on one extreme or the other. To detect small differences in self-knowledge between persons, or growth of self-knowledge in persons over a period of time, requires controlled observation.

As Seen by Others

One means of controlling observation is to train it. A competent psychotherapist is usually able to estimate a person's degree of self-awareness by what he says about himself and how he says it. That which is seen by the clinically trained eye but not by the subject himself provides one index of self-knowledge. Holt [47] used a diagnostic council of ten psychologists for such a comparison. Each subject was seen by each member of the council for approximately four hours. The council members then rated the subject on 148 personal traits, met to discuss and resolve their differences, and compared their ratings with those made by the subject himself. The difference between the council's rating of the subject and the subject's rating of himself for each trait was taken as his measure of self-knowledge.

When a group of subjects know themselves well enough to observe and rate one another knowledgeably, professional training is less important. The writer[48] had groups of five to seven college students rate one another and themselves on twelve descriptive statements taken from the previous chapter (section II). Three of these groups (from campus "covenant communities") professed a particular religious orientation and three (from fraternities) did not. The results showed that the covenant community members came closer to describing themselves as their peers saw them than did the fraternity members.

Unfortunately, the simplicity of design and administration does not extend to scoring and interpretation. The size of a difference between two views of a person does not necessarily reflect the degree of self-awareness and insight. A simple discrepancy score such as this often fails to take account of observer stereotypes, personal friendships, easy and difficult "target" persons, use of scale differences, and other possibly biasing factors built into the rating situation. Sound statistical methods can minimize the danger of some, but not all, of these. Despite such difficulties, however, the method has been widely used and has proved its value.

Accuracy of the "Projected" Self

A different approach to the measurement of self-knowledge employs a variant of standard projective techniques. In one design reported by Grossman,[49] Thematic Apperception Test (TAT) pictures suggesting aggression, sexuality, and parental figures were viewed by subjects instructed to select the most probable explanation for, or outcome of, each scene. On the theory that a person will not attribute to a projection that of which he has no awareness in himself, Grossman had two clinical psychologists rate each possible response for the degree of insight shown. A nonpictorial adaptation of this design is described by Tolor and Reznikoff.[50] The authors formulated twenty-seven hypothetical situations depicting the use of common defenses. The subject was asked to explain the described behavior by selecting the most likely and the least likely of four listed explanatory statements. Prior weighting of these items by judges was then compared with the subject's own rating to determine his insight score.

The worth of these two related designs rests in large part upon the presumption that social perception is a function of self-perception and that the person who is unable to understand the motives of others cannot understand or acknowledge his own. These experimenters assume a hierarchy of "correct" insights for all subjects to which the individual selections of each subject are compared. For example, if the subject fails to see that a certain pictured or described paternal relationship is laden with unexpressed hostility, he is scored as unaware of his own conflicts in this area. There seems to be ample clinical evidence to support this theory, including thousands of hours in personal therapy spent each year by student psychotherapists who might otherwise overlook conflicts in the lives of their patients by remaining unaware of their own.

Avoiding the Observer's Bias

It is sometimes objected that measures of self-knowledge like the four already discussed cannot really compare what a person knows about himself with the truth about himself, since this "truth" is always a guess. Another's opinion of a subject may err as much as the subject's opinion of himself. The objection has merit, if only to caution us that trained or collective personality estimates are still subjective estimates. The subjective element can be effectively minimized by sound observation and rating procedures, but even the best controls cannot transform a necessarily subjective criterion into an essentially objective one.

It is useful, therefore, to have at hand a number of measures employing objective criteria. While as a rule these "objective" measures tap a narrower range of personality traits than those just considered, they can provide a valuable check on the accuracy of the more comprehensive "subjective" measures. In a study reported by Cottrell,[51] students were asked to make academic self-evaluations on the basis of earned grade-point averages. By the laws of chance it would be expected that over a three- or four-year period as many poor grades would be forgotten or mistaken as good grades. The fact that some students forgot nearly equal numbers of poor and good grades (defined by their individual averages) while others decidedly favored their good grades demonstrates real differences in self-knowledge.

In the same way that an academic grade can represent an important segment of a student's personal history and self-image, so also can a person's self-evaluation at one moment in time be used as a base line to assess his self-knowledge on a subsequent occasion. Gergen[52] had male subjects rate themselves on seventy-two personal traits. Fifty-six subjects whose ratings were neither extremely self-approving nor self-depreciating were interviewed for thirty minutes by an attractive female. The interviewer readministered the rating scale orally, smiling or nodding each time a subject awarded himself a more socially desirable rating than before. A post-interview questionnaire asked each subject to estimate the degree to which he had changed his self-concept, in which direction, by how much, and the cause of the change. The value of this design is demonstrated by the fact that those who had changed their self-concepts the least tended to be most aware of the changes they had made and most aware of the interviewer's influence on these changes.

Recalling What Hurts

The particular aspect of self-knowledge that has received the most attention in experimental literature has to do with the recall of painful or threatening experiences. Some of these designs show refreshing imagination and realism. For instance, Sanford and Risser[53] tested twenty-five mothers in their homes in the presence of a teen-age daughter. The mothers were given plastic pieces of different shapes and asked to use them in making designs similar to those printed on a card. To create a high degree of involvement with the task, their daughters were instructed to watch their mothers' performances carefully. Mothers were purposely failed on six of fifteen designs, and scored on the proportion of successes to failures later recalled. While some mothers remembered as many failures as successes, most remembered more successes. On a retest four months later no significant differences between recalled successes and failures were found, suggesting that during the four-month interlude the threat of these failure experiences was softened by accomplishments in other areas of life.

In another type of social situation, Harvey[54] had groups of subjects interact and then rate one another on socially salient characteristics. Instead of the actual ratings made of him, each subject was shown fictitious ratings prepared in advance at one of five levels of disparagement. A few minutes later subjects were asked to recall the ratings they had received. Some subjects remembered (or forgot) their ratings regardless of what they were, but most did not. The majority showed that the more unfavorable the rating, the greater the tendency to make an error in recall.

Emotionally disturbing words are often used in tests of recall too. Levinger and Clark[55] presented subjects with thirty emotionally disturbing words and thirty neutral words used about as frequently and asked them to respond with the first word that came to mind. When the list of sixty words was read again, subjects were asked to recall their prior response to each word. Of the thirty-four subjects, thirty-one forgot more associations to emotionally disturbing words than to neutral words. Only three persons forgot equal numbers of disturbing and neutral associations, illustrating the rigor of the technique. "Fear," "angry," and "love" led the least-recalled list while "head," "fur," and "lake" were among the most recalled by association. The degree of perceived threat posed by each word was checked by the association time and amount of skin resistance to the flow of electricity (GSR).

The propensity to forget that which is emotionally disturbing extends even to emotionally neutral words after exposure to a threatening situation. D'Zurilla[56] had subjects learn twenty neutral words and tested them for recall. The group was then given a Rorschach-type inkblot test and asked to pick one of two previously learned words "that best expresses the meaning for each blot." Ten inkblots were shown in all. Half the subjects were given the impression that the inkblot test was designed to spot homosexual tendencies and half were not. After another recall test the subjects under homosexual instructions were individually told that they had picked a predominance of "homosexual words." A third recall test was administered, the hoax was revealed, and a final recall test was given. The results showed no recall differences between the two groups on the first and last tests, but a significant difference between them on the second and third tests. This dramatic restoration of memory for threat-associated words (by the mere removal of the threatening situation that occasioned the forgetting) provides an ingenious double check by which persons who do and do not lose awareness of emotionally disturbing events can be distinguished.

How Valid Are These Selective Recall Tests?

It is well to note that the principle of selective recall embodied by these last six reported designs is not all there is to self-knowledge, at least not obviously so. While it may be true that a number of these designs come quite close to specifying some of the actual conditions in which some persons remember and others forget personally relevant facts, the degree to which we are justified in claiming that experimental selective recall is "similar" to the whole range of life situations in which self-knowledge is involved depends upon two things.

The first of these concerns what it is that is remembered

or forgotten. Most research to date has used words and other verbal symbols to represent life situations. Yet in one experimental situation cited (Sanford and Risser) tactile and perceptual designs were recalled. In two others[57] subjects were asked to recall possibly threatening pictures. There are other designs[58] in which words take on threatening connotations by virtue of their immediate association with a threatening situation. From this it appears that it is the properties of the life situation, and not of the word that represents it, which account for the forgetting.

The second thing needed to justify the selective recall design has to do with the nature of the perceived threat. It must be representative of those threats to safety, security, and self-esteem described in the previous section. Here again there is something to go on. Published experimental designs embody the threat of social rejection,[59] of task failure in the context of home and family,[60] of sexual and aggressive stimuli,[61] of mental deficiency and academic failure,[62] of physical pain,[63] and of various unstructured or ambiguous situations.[64] Despite apparent outward dissimilarities, all these types of threats proved significantly related to recall ability. In at least three designs reported in recent years[65] this association was further demonstrated by the restoration of experimentally diminished recall ability.

The variety found among types of threatening situations as well as among things forgotten is thus considerably greater than the reading of one or two reports might suggest. There can be little question that many of the threatening situations used in these research designs can strike close to the heart of a person's sense of security, especially that not securely grounded throughout the entire personality. It may not be so obvious that a defective recall of threatening material corresponds to the same lack of insight, awareness, and self-knowledge of which theologians speak.

In this light the problem becomes simply whether that which is forgotten under threat is central or peripheral to self-knowledge. On the surface it is difficult to make a case for the centrality of a word, a picture, a task, or even a limited repertoire of life situations. Ultimately no convincing case can be made short of actually broadening the scope of present research designs to include just those situations which now seem to raise questions of applicability. But between these two extremes there seems to be some logic (although finally circular) in contending that *whatever* is selectively forgotten as a result of confrontation with an experimentally simulated life threat is central to insight and self-knowledge. This step requires a psychological inference. But since it is the inference that made possible modern depth psychology, the risk is not great.

IV

That Uneasy Feeling

Having begun this chapter with a Protestant view of self-knowledge embodied by the man of faith, you may have arrived at this point with some genuine misgivings. Were my steps from theology to actual testing situations direct? Would Luther, Kierkegaard, Barth, and Tillich, for example, feel satisfied that the measures described in these pages get to the heart of their thought?

I think not—at least not immediately. But this is not a bad thing. Were you—or Luther—to assent to the implied "theological validity" of these measures on the basis of the printed words above, I would have some misgivings too. For until one puts himself into a particular testing situation as a subject or as the experimenter (preferably both), there is no real way to get the sense of its theological relevance—or irrelevance.

The final test of an empirical test is not empirical, or even logical, but simply whether it "speaks to" your theological sensibilities in the midst of test-taking and test-giving. You must be the judge.

NOTES

1. Barth, IV/2, 283; cf. Bonhoeffer, *Ethics*, p. 250.
2. H. Richard Niebuhr, *Revelation*, p. 18; cf. *Responsible Self*, p. 48; Bultmann, *Existence and Faith*, p. 221; Kierkegaard, *For Self-examination*, pp. 38, 51.
3. Bultmann, *Essays*, pp. 48, 94; Reinhold Niebuhr, *Nature*, pp. 124-25.
4. Bonhoeffer, *Cost of Discipleship*, p. 186; cf. Tillich, *Systematic Theology*, III, 231-32; Kierkegaard, *Postscript*, p. 78.
5. Barth III/4, 672, 674; Bonhoeffer, *Letters and Papers*, pp. 159-60.
6. Bultmann, *Essays*, p. 94; cf. Tillich, *Protestant Era*, pp. 115-16; Bonhoeffer, *Letters and Papers*, pp. 159-60; Luther, *Galatians 1-4*, p. 49.
7. H. Richard Niebuhr, *Revelation*, pp. 84-85; Bonhoeffer, *Letters and Papers*, pp. 159-60.
8. Tillich, *Protestant Era*, pp. 115-16; cf. H. Richard Niebuhr, *Revelation*, p. 18; cf. *Responsible Self*, p. 48; *Revelation*, p. 114.
9. Barth, III/4, 500; cf. Bultmann, *Existence and Faith*, p. 180; Bonhoeffer, *Letters and Papers*, pp. 159-60.
10. Bultmann, *Essays*, p. 233; cf. Barth, III/4, 665.
11. Barth, IV/2, 283; cf. Luther, *Galatians 1-4*, p. 37; Bultmann, *Essays*, pp. 48-49; Bonhoeffer, *Ethics*, p. 250.
12. Bultmann, *Essays*, p. 94; cf. Tillich, *Protestant Era*, pp. 115-16.
13. Luther, *Galatians 1-4*, p. 37; cf. Bonhoeffer, *Ethics*, p. 48; Bultmann, *Essays*, pp. 48-49.
14. Tillich, *Protestant Era*, p. 73; cf. Luther, *Galatians 1-4*, p. 288; Schleiermacher, *On Religion*, p. 41; Bonhoeffer, *Ethics*, p. 203; Kierkegaard, *Postscript*, p. 151; Calvin, *Institutes*, ii.8, 3.
15. Luther, *Galatians 5-6*, p. 70.
16. Kierkegaard, *Fear and Trembling*, p. 54; *Postscript*, p. 130; Barth, III/4, 588-89; H. Richard Niebuhr, *Revelation*, pp. 113-14.
17. Kierkegaard, *Postscript*, p. 538, cf. p. 131.
18. Kierkegaard, *Fear and Trembling*, p. 110; cf. Bultmann, *Essays*, p. 96; Tillich, *Protestant Era*, p. 73; Luther, *Galatians 5-6*, p. 70.
19. Tillich, *Shaking of the Foundations*, pp. 43-44; Kierkegaard, *Postscript*, pp. 78, 431; Calvin, *Institutes*, iii.8, 3, Reinhold Niebuhr, *Destiny*, pp. 43, 125-26.
20. Bultmann, *Essays*, pp. 48-49; cf. Bonhoeffer, *Letters and Papers*, pp. 209-10.
21. Tillich, *Systematic Theology*, III, 231; cf. Luther, *Galatians 5-6*, p. 74; Tillich, *Shaking of the Foundations*. pp. 56-57.
22. Bultmann, *Essays*, pp. 53, 94.
23. Kierkegaard, *Postscript*, p. 316.
24. Bultmann, *Essays*, p. 64; cf. Calvin, *Institutes*, iii.3, 18; H. Richard Niebuhr, *Revelation*, pp. 113-14.
25. Kierkegaard, *Postscript*, p. 431; cf. Bonhoeffer, *Ethics*, p. 203; Schleiermacher, *On Religion*, p. 243.

26. Barth, III/4, 672; Tillich, *Systematic Theology*, III, 231; Bultmann, *Essays*, pp. 48-49; Bonhoeffer, *Ethics*, p. 250.

27. Mark 9:14-24.

28. Calvin, *Institutes*, ii.1, 2; Bultmann, *Kerygma and Myth*, p. 31; H. Richard Niebuhr, *Revelation*, pp. 101-2.

29. Rudolf Bultmann, *Primitive Christianity in Its Contemporary Setting*, trans. R. H. Fuller (Meridian Books; Cleveland: World, 1956), p. 189; Bonhoeffer, *Cost of Discipleship*, pp. 212-13; Reinhold Niebuhr, *Nature*, pp. 121, 130-31; Schleiermacher, *Christian Faith*, p. 509.

30. Mark 14:31, 66-72.

31. I Sam. 26:1–27:1; cf. I Sam. 24.

32. Tillich, *Shaking of the Foundations*, pp. 43-44; cf. Kierkegaard, *Works of Love*, p. 195; Schleiermacher, *Christian Faith*, pp. 311-12.

33. Luke 15:29.

34. Kierkegaard, *Works of Love*, p. 195; cf. *Postscript*, p. 538; H. Richard Niebuhr, *Revelation*, pp. 113-14.

35. Bonhoeffer, *Cost of Discipleship*, pp. 212-13, cf. Bultmann, *Primitive Christianity*, p. 189; Kierkegaard, *Works of Love*, p. 195.

36. Reinhold Niebuhr, *Nature*, pp. 36, 121; cf. Luther, *Galatians 1-4*, p. 49; Kierkegaard, *For Self-examination*, pp. 38, 51; Bultmann, *Existence and Faith*, p. 180; Richard Niebuhr, *Revelation*, pp. 113-14.

37. Luther, *Galatians 1-4*, pp. 35, 49; Calvin, *Institutes*, i.1, 2; cf. Bultmann, *Essays*, p. 48; Bonhoeffer, *Life Together*, p. 110.

38. Luke 18:10-13.

39. Bultmann, *Existence and Faith*, p. 180; cf. Kierkegaard, *For Self-examination*, p. 50; Tillich, *Shaking of the Foundations*, pp. 56-57; Bultmann, *Essays*, p. 48; Bonhoeffer, *Life Together*, pp. 110-13.

40. II Sam. 12:1-6.

41. Tillich, *Protestant Era*, p. 171; Kierkegaard, *For Self-examination*, p. 50; Reinhold Niebuhr, *Destiny*, pp. 215, 225.

42. II Sam. 12:7-10.

43. Kierkegaard, *Fear and Trembling*, p. 57; cf. Bonhoeffer, *Cost of Discipleship*, p. 189; Reinhold Niebuhr, *Destiny*, pp. 320-21; Bultmann, *Existence and Faith*, pp. 85-86; Tillich, *Shaking of the Foundations*, p. 59.

44. Barth, III/2, 47; IV/2, 416-17; Kierkegaard, *Fear and Trembling*, p. 54; cf. H. Richard Niebuhr, *Revelation*, pp. 113-14.

45. Calvin, *Institutes*, ii.1, 2; Reinhold Niebuhr, *Destiny*, p. 225; H. Richard Niebuhr, *Revelation*, pp. 113-14.

46. Barth, III/4, 588-89; IV/2, 379; cf. III/4, 43; Bultmann, *Existence and Faith*, p. 180.

47. Robert R. Holt, "The Accuracy of Self-evaluation: Its Measurement and Some of Its Personological Correlates," *Journal of Consulting Psychology*, XV (1951), 95-101.

48. David C. Duncombe, "The Evaluation of University Covenant Communities: A Critique and a Proposal," report prepared for the Danforth Study of Campus Ministries, 1965, and published in extract as "An Experiment in Evaluation of Faith and Life Communities," in *The Church, the University and Social Policy*, ed. Kenneth Underwood (Middletown, Conn.: Wesleyan University Press, 1969), III.

49. David Grossman, "The Construction and Validation of Two Insight Inventories," *Journal of Consulting Psychology*, XV (1951), 109-14.

50. Alexander Tolor and Marvin Reznikoff, "A New Approach to Insight: A Preliminary Report," *Journal of Nervous and Mental Disease*, CXXX (1960), 286-96.

51. Nickolas B. Cottrell, "The Measurement of Unwarranted Self-evaluative Behavior," *Dissertation Abstracts*, XXV (1964), 1378.

52. Kenneth J. Gergen, "The Effects of Interaction Goals and Personalistic Feedback on the Presentation of the Self," *Journal of Personality and Social Psychology*, I (1965), 413-24.

53. Nevitt Sanford and Joseph Risser, "What Are the Conditions of Self-defensive Forgetting?" *Journal of Personality*, XVII (1949), 244-60.

54. O. J. Harvey, "Personality Factors in Resolution of Conceptual Incongruities," *Sociometry*, XXV (1962), 336-52.

55. George Levinger and James Clark, "Emotional Factors in the Forgetting of Word Associations," *Journal of Abnormal and Social Psychology*, LXI (1961), 99-105.

56. Thomas D'Zurilla, "Recall Efficiency and Mediating Cognitive Events in 'Experimental Repression,' " *Journal of Personality and Social Psychology*, I (1965), 253-57.

57. Milton Rokeach, "Attitude as a Determinant of Distortions in Recall," *Journal of Abnormal and Social Psychology*, XLVII (1952), 482-88; Sidney I. Perloe, "Inhibition as a Determinant of Perceptual Defense," *Perceptual and Motor Skills*, XI (1960), 59-66.

58. Charles W. Eriksen, "Defense Against Ego-Threat in Memory and Perception," *Journal of Abnormal and Social Psychology*, XLVII (1952), 230-35; Anchard F. Zeller, "An Experimental Analogue of Repression: II. The Effect of Individual Failure and Success on Memory Measured by Learning," *Journal of Experimental Psychology*, XL (1950), 411-22; Richard S. Lazarus and Nicholas Longo, "The Consistency of Psychological Defenses Against Threat," *Journal of Abnormal and Social Psychology*, XLVIII (1953), 495-99; M. R. D'Amato and W. E. Gumenik, "Some Effects of Immediate Versus Delayed Shock on an Instrumental Response and Cognitive Processes," *Journal of Abnormal and Social Psychology*, LX (1960), 64-67; John Lowenfield, "Negative Affect as a Causal Factor in the Occurrence of Repression, Subception, and Perceptual Defense," *Journal of Personality*, XXIX (1961), 54-63.

59. Harvey, "Personality Factors in Resolution of Conceptual Incongruities."

60. Sanford and Risser, "What Are the Conditions of Self-defensive Forgetting?"

61. Perloe, "Inhibition as a Determinant of Perceptual Defense"; D'Zurilla, "Recall Efficiency in Mediating Cognitive Events in 'Experimental Repression' "; Rokeach, "Attitude as a Determinant of Distortions in Recall."

62. Zeller, "An Experimental Analogue of Repression: II. The Effect of Individual Failure and Success on Memory Measured by Learning."

63. D'Amato and Gumenik, "Some Effects of Immediate Versus Delayed Shock on an Instrumental Response and Cognitive Processes."

64. Else Frenkel-Brunswik, "Intolerance of Ambiguity as an Emotional and Perceptual Personality Variable," *Journal of Personality*, XVIII (1949-

50), 108-43; Desmond S. Cartwright, "Self-consistency as a Factor Affecting Immediate Recall," *Journal of Abnormal and Social Psychology*, LII (1956), 212-18.

65. D'Zurilla, "Recall Efficiency and Mediating Cognitive Events in 'Experimental Repression' "; Zeller, "An Experimental Analogue of Repression: II. The Effect of Individual Failure and Success on Memory Measured by Learning"; Charles B. Truax, "The Repression Response to Implied Failure as a Function of the Hysteria-Psychasthenia Index," *Journal of Abnormal and Social Psychology*, LV (1957), 188-93.

chapter IV

BEING ONESELF

I

The Roots of Honest Expression in Protestant Thought

The mature Christian can express his feelings and thoughts as honestly as he faces them. It is not enough that he see himself truthfully; he must reveal himself to others with the same frankness. Why this is so becomes clear when we look at certain assumptions underlying Christian thought.

Implied by Self-knowledge

From the beginning the Christian church has understood itself to be a fellowship of clay-footed mortals in whom the power of Christ is at work. It sees itself as the "body of Christ" having many "members." [1] Hence, one's identity as a Christian involves the identity of the fellowship too. What he "is" does not end with himself, but extends into —and is drawn from—the lives of his fellow Christians. In practical terms this means that unless individual Christians are able to reveal themselves to one another in an honest and forthright way, they have no common knowledge of who or what they are as a Christian fellowship. It is in this sense that genuine self-knowledge and self-expression, although distinguishable, imply one another in Christian thought.

There is another sense in which this is true as well. Openness among persons often enables deeper individual self-awareness. The age-old practice of confession has shown that Christians realize about themselves only as much as they reveal of themselves. Knowledge of the self not only enables confession, but is deepened by it. To know oneself is to be known, and to be known requires an honest expression of one's heartfelt desires, feelings, doubts, and thoughts. Theologians imply just this when they speak of "acknowledging" something about oneself, i.e., admitting it both inwardly and outwardly.[2] In practice, self-awareness and self-expression go together, and certainly both are understood to be necessary for the reception of saving grace.

The Hippie Hedge

Nevertheless, the particular place of honest expression in the Christian life is still debated. Many theologians, Protestants among them, support the principle of radical openness yet condemn certain expressions of it. For example, Calvin describes the Christian as one who will "repress the tickling wantonness" that leads to "vicious and hurtful speculation" and one who should "willingly remain hedged in" by "boundaries" that "enclose our minds."[3] As Christians, he says, we will "regulate our minds and tongues, so as never to think or speak of God and his mysteries without reverence and great soberness" nor have any "feeling toward him" except that of "deep veneration."[4] Even when disaster overtakes the Christian, he does not "murmur against God" but will "maintain his confidence in him" with a "placid and grateful mind." [5]

Calvin may represent something of an extreme, but few Protestant theologians are without fear that honest expression may lead to impiety or license. The specter of the libertine giving free rein to his thoughts and desires—or the prospect of social chaos and religious doubt sweeping Christendom —qualifies many a theologian's zeal for liberally applying the principle of honest expression to the specifics of the Christian life. Yet the theologian is compelled by his own understanding of the biblical faith to radically affirm the basis of human self-expression since it touches the heart of at least two fundamental Protestant doctrines: creation and redemption.

The Protestant Principle

According to the doctrine of creation, God affirms human life, impulse, and vitality. Creatureliness, in all its physical, emotional, and rational dimensions, is seen as the intended condition of man. The goodness of creation means that man can acknowledge his creatureliness without shame or suppression. Not to acknowledge one's creatureliness presumes a higher wisdom or goodness than that of creation itself. In fact, it is this presumption, the presumption of godliness by which man seeks to negate his created goodness, that justifies shame and suppression of human vitality. Insofar as human expression reflects that which God gives man and not man's effort to change or deny it, the expression is to be affirmed. The difficulty of course is in distinguishing between the two when at the practical level there is often no way of separating them.

Perhaps even more centrally related to honest expression than the doctrine of creation is the Protestant understanding of redemption. This is because it cuts through the practical dilemma of trying to express created goodness without its inevitable human corruptions. When united with the full humanity of the crucified and risen Christ, both the uncorrupted and the corrupted elements of life can be openly expressed. This does not mean license for unbridled expression of the passions, but it does mean that even the worst in oneself can be revealed without fear of divine condemnation. The person in whom Christ is at work experiences the sense of being accepted despite the corruptions of his heart. In Christ, God recognizes a man just as he is and enables him to do the same. It is the essence of the so-called Protestant principle that all things are pure in Christ. This means that no form of true self-expression is alien to the man whose justification is by God's grace alone, and only in such a man can self-expression be genuine and honest.

An Emerging Focus

Like self-knowledge, honest expression has undergone a gradual change of emphasis in Protestantism. To the reformers confession of sins and knowledge of one's sins were intimately connected with forgiveness and saving faith. The pages of their works ring with charges of papist hypocrisy, dishonesty, and deceit before God and man so it is not unwarranted to suggest a decided polemic interest in honest expression. Seen also in the writings of early Protestants is their support for open expression of feelings in song and prayer, especially feelings of sorrow, contrition, praise, and thanksgiving. Yet for all this, a pietistic pall hangs over the boldest manifestos of inner honesty. A full-bodied concern for the pleasures and sorrows of earthly life was often taken as a sign of spiritual weakness, to be expressed in a spirit of contrition rather than by feelings of pleasure and sorrow.

Perhaps because contemporary Protestant theologians have less need to guard against the libertine interpretations of Reformation manifestos or the moral laxness and sacrilegious practices of a medieval church, Protestant thought is becoming bolder in its approach to honest expression. Using the great Reformation themes sharpened by the insights of depth psychology, modern theology has shown itself better able to distinguish between honest expression and expression that is essentially shallow, insincere, or destructive. The effect has been to shift the focus of theological interest toward those areas of human existence most basic to the ongoing emotional life of the Christian. Contemporary theologians, by affirming the full humanity of created and redeemed man, have opened the way for a better look at the expression of such basic feelings as anger, lust, doubt, and enjoyment of earthy satisfactions. The description to follow reflects this trend, expecially where the trend supports concretely the major doctrinal concerns of the reformers.

II

With Nothing to Hide

There is a kind of person who can simply "be" himself.[6] He lives fully and freely, not cautiously. He expresses his feelings and thoughts with "radical openness." When the occasion demands, he can reveal himself honestly and with utter candor.[7] Yet his freedom is not that of the libertine. His expression is natural, reflecting the depth of his feelings; it is meant neither to stimulate nor exhibit his feelings.[8] Rather he is distinguished by the way in which he seems at ease with himself and others. Even in circumstances of great personal concern or threat he can express what he genuinely feels at the moment in a frank and disarming way.[9] He has nothing to hide.

Out of the Depths

Such openness reaches into every area of his life but perhaps most noticeably where we "truly feel our wants" and have a "sincere, nay, ardent desire of obtaining them." [10] Yearnings for a carefree existence, the open road, a great challenge, the simple beauty and contentment of rural life, or the richness and stimulation of the city he can acknowledge as part of himself. Whatever cries out of the depths, however visionary and unrealizable, he will not deny before others. The hopes and the aspirations that infuse his life and give it meaning he wears as comfortably as his weathered fishing hat.

Nor will that which weighs heavily upon him remain hidden from view. "To bear the cross patiently is not to have your feelings altogether blunted." As his life is touched by death, worry, or misfortune, he reveals a good bit of what he feels.[11] Like Jesus in Gethsemane he is able to face the deepest crisis, unashamedly admitting his distress and expressing his desire that the "hour might pass from him." [12] On the night that his son is killed in an automobile accident he goes through a hell of seething emotions. His grief swells and breaks forth, one moment in sobbing, another moment in cursing, and still another moment in prayer. By word, gesture, and silence he pours out his feelings to his family and friends and has theirs poured upon him. Nothing is held back save by discretion or exhaustion. Emotion is expressed as it is felt: pain, sorrow, anger, fear, love, and guilt—all "heartfelt utterances made during storms." [13] And if these feelings are also mingled with despair and doubt, he is able to cry out with Jesus on the cross: "My God, my God, why hast thou forsaken me?" [14]

Expressing the Commonplace

Such openness extends beyond times of crisis and the expression of basic emotions. The mature Christian is as honest about the day-to-day concerns. If the cares of the world that rest upon his shoulders seem lighter, it is because he can talk about them. Perhaps he sees himself going nowhere in his chosen line of work or wonders whether he will always be saddled with payments that leave nothing at the end of the month. Business risks, a chronically sick child, a noisy transmission in the family car constantly remind him of trouble ahead. Yet it is the freedom with which he can express, or not express, "the wrestling of the human spirit" that characterizes the Christian way of life.[15]

Some of these expressible worries may have to do with personal failures and shortcomings. Here the element of embarrassment often limits how honest we are. It is not an easy thing to own up to something that violates one's own self-expectations or the expectations of others. The person whose convictions, status, or profession demands the highest integrity is often tempted to conceal his fallibility. In some instances he will be wise to do so.[16] To confess an instance of poor judgment to a medical colleague may be a sign of real strength, but the same confession to a patient before an operation may show little more than a propensity for poor judgment. Here too it is the all-important sense of security that allows one to reveal or conceal the worst about himself as the situation warrants. Because the Christian has no inner need to see himself as a god, he can accept his human shortcomings and admit them with appropriate feelings of regret, guilt, and contrition. He will "speak sincerely and frankly, and make a clean breast" of this weakness.[17]

Yet with this comes a certain abandon and "undisguised

egoism." [18] Not only does he have the strength to speak of his failures, but he will speak openly of his successes. Like the apostle Paul, he can throw caution to the winds and "boast" of his feats without embarrassment.[19] If something worthy of admiration has been done, he shows no less enthusiasm because of his own part in it. It is a victory to be celebrated, and he can do it with the unselfconscious abandon of David, who went "leaping and dancing before the Lord" as the ark was led into Jerusalem.[20]

Such a person gives unaffected expression to his joy. He takes pleasure and "delight" in the common things of life but knows also how to give fitting expression to the uncommon.[21] When good fortune comes his way, he is not one to feel guilty about enjoying it. If he can afford it—and sometimes when he can't—he is capable of splurging a whole week's paycheck without regret on a skiing weekend or a night on the town. Perhaps there is a touch of madness in what he does, for when he feels like letting go and celebrating life, he deems himself accountable only to those who share his inner freedom. The intensity and expression of the delight that he knows spring from the depth of his soul and are not lessened by their momentary nature.

Feelings About People: Anger and Affection

In one way or another all genuine expression reflects what we feel with or about other people. Even the joy known in solitude is something shared with others at certain times. Yet not all expression reflects the same degree of emotional involvement with people. Feelings arising out of frustrating human relationships, for instance, are among the most powerful that we experience. Largely for this reason the manner in which these feelings are expressed is often highly indicative of how genuinely free a person is to express himself openly.

When the Christian has been crossed or blocked by someone, he shows it. He gets angry. You can see it in the way he acts and by what he says. "Violent utterances," "accusations," and even "blasphemy" can be appropriate.[22] Like Jesus with the temple merchants, he may lash out with words and blows when he feels he is in the right.[23] And if his frustrater is not at hand, he may ventilate his feelings of anger by swearing or slamming some object. Yet he can go on from there to seek out others—his frustrater among them if possible—to tell them how he feels. Whatever bitterness and hatred he finds in his heart he is able to reveal when discretion allows, even if his hearers are the superiors he obeys or the authorities he respects. Whether knowingly or not, his anger is expressed in a way that seems best to remove the frustration, clear the air, and restore or improve his relations with others.

Feelings arising out of satisfying human relationships are sometimes as difficult to reveal as those known in frustrating circumstances. The freedom of the Christian allows him to express his "earthly affection" for others as he feels it, without need for apology or excuse.[24] For instance, he feels no embarrassment in asking someone he likes to spend the time of day with him and can show or speak of his affection in a genuine and unrehearsed manner. Nor is he embarrassed to show his dependence upon those whose friendship means the most.

With the person he loves he experiences the intimacy between man and woman without shame or pretense. He "allows the flood of life to flow freely" and regards "bodily joys" as an "end" in themselves.[25] Yet the Christian man is capable of deep and meaningful friendships with other women too and can genuinely express his affection for them. When strong sexual desires are mingled with this affection, he is more likely to speak directly of these feelings to persons other than those involved, for reasons of discretion and safety. This is not prudishness. He feels no guilt over momentary sexual desires and fantasies. "Carnal desires" and "sexual passion" are accepted "as far as they are natural." He recognizes these to be true expressions of his own sexuality and can talk or joke about them without needing to use many-syllabled words.[26] The difference between the Christian and the libertine is not that the Christian feels or expresses fewer sexual desires, but that he is not driven to act on them. Attracted by the woman next door, he need not seduce her or in some subtle way arouse her sexual feelings. Honest expression is not calculated implementation.

The same holds true for family members or friends of the same sex. Like the biblical Ruth or Jonathan, the Christian risks deep attachments for the joy of friendship.[27] These attachments may also give rise to sexual desires, but he is not frightened by them. Rather, he allows his feelings of need and love to express themselves in whatever way seems fitting. At times this may be no more than a warm smile or friendly gesture. But there will be other times when his feelings are more naturally expressed by a word of affection and devotion, in an emotional embrace, or by a touch of the hand. To family and friends of either sex for whom he has a special affection he is able to show his feelings openly without fear or embarrassment.

Even Conflicting Feelings

Though he may feel the weight of one such emotion so intensely that for a time nothing else can be expressed, the mature Christian is able also to give "rich and full" expression to the entire range of his feelings.[28] He can openly acknowledge the degree to which his friendships, his marriage, and his work afford both satisfaction and frustration. If he has done a thing worthy of shame or remorse, he will be able to confess genuine sorrow and yet at the same time express the joy or pleasure it may also have brought. As a man of deep but often conflicting passions and "opposite" moods, he "can make room for conflicting emotions at the same time." He is able to show both his hostility and his love toward those closest to him. Because of his "anger" he will not "suppress his filial piety." [29] Like Jeremiah he can lift his voice and shout, "Sing to the Lord; praise the Lord!" and in the next breath cry, "Cursed be the day on which I was born!" [30]

Whatever the feeling or thought, no matter how deeply it touches or confuses his life, the Christian has nothing to hide. To the most important inner experiences he adds nothing more than appropriate expression.

Behind the Mask

At the other extreme is the man who fears revealing his true self. He has acquired the habit of watching himself carefully lest he show an undesirable trait. This manner is especially apparent under stress or in the company of those to whom he looks for acceptance and approval. It is as though he were saying to himself: "If they only knew what I'm really like." Although racked by doubts of personal worth and competence, he is unable to express them.[31]

All Bottled Up

What he does express varies with the person. Some people express little of anything. Their whole manner is one of constrictedness or "suppression," of holding in check all activity and impulse beyond that needed to carry on routine daily tasks.[32] They appear to be humorless, listless, sexless, lifeless, and cautious. Such a person will often visibly tighten when confronted by a situation that threatens to stimulate his feelings or deprive him of control. He may not even be aware of his "bottled up" feelings,[33] although they are uncommonly strong and are usually of a sexual or aggressive nature. Perhaps the only thing he does feel and express openly, beyond a drab oneness of emotion, is an underlying sense of anxiety, guilt, or apprehension. It is an though he were aware that beneath the calm, almost dead exterior lies a powder keg of emotion that can be ignited by the slightest spark.

The eccentric is often this kind of person. People generally recognize, accept, and "understand" eccentrics without questions or offense. The protection given by this understanding allows a more direct and exaggerated expression of his constrictedness. The eccentric's odd mannerisms and living habits allow little opportunity for direct emotional expression and steer him away from chance encounters with emotionally upsetting situations. Since he is expected to express himself unnaturally—and experiences a certain amount of social approval for doing so—the eccentric way of life removes the imminent danger of having his deeper feelings unexpectedly exposed.

An interesting variant of this is the person who expresses the opposite of what he feels. He employs "masks" or "camouflages," often unknowingly.[34] If he is angry at someone, he may smile and act friendly. Those he vents his wrath upon are often persons for whom he experiences an unacceptable sexual attraction. Still another variation is a "new kind of Stoics, who hold it vicious not only to groan and weep, but even to be sad and anxious." [35] These people may be remarkably aware of their feelings, yet they can do nothing more than dispassionately discuss them. They are incapable of imparting any true feeling to either their words or their actions yet often think of themselves as highly sensitive and expressive individuals.

However there is another way of burying one's feelings, more subtle and effective than any of these—if practiced in moderation. The person committing himself to this form of deception chooses to give reasons for the poverty of his expression. Modesty, decency, propriety, self-control, and piety are among his most potent arguments or forms of justification. He assumes the role of the distinguished, reserved, perhaps slightly conservative pillar of society. Since a person of stature is not supposed to experience the baser emotions of life, he knows that he is not expected to express them. He knows also that even were he to experience such emotions or to have a number of embarrassing faults, it would be considered a lack of common decency to express them. He deems it proper to "suppress vitality for the sake of the spirit." [36] With an arsenal of reasons to justify his lack of appropriate expression, he will present an unruffled front to the world and count undisciplined expression a sign of weakness. He is often quite believable, even to himself.

The Unbottled Libertine

Every method of concealing genuine feeling is, of course, a disguise. One of the most deceiving of these is that worn by the "libertine," the person who affects a public show of his inner life.[37] The style he assumes may be that of the extrovert, the teller of racy jokes and off-color stories, or the accomplished Don Juan. Then again it may be that of the confessor who manipulates his prey by revealing secret confidences. Both forms reflect more an estimate of others' vulnerabilities than they express genuine personal feelings. While outwardly resembling the person capable of honest expression in many respects, the libertine may be distinguished by the shallowness and inflexibility of his expression. Both may tell the same racy jokes or reveal the same inner secrets, but the Christian can do it or not do it according to how well it reflects his feelings and fits the situation. Lacking this sensitivity, the deceiver wears a "mask" frozen in one expression and is literally driven to play the role of the libertine extrovert or confidant for fear of revealing his true self.[38]

Concealing His Thoughts

The expression of feeling is not the only thing affected by the "dread of being oneself." When a person hides his feelings, he will also hide certain thoughts, especially those which might cause others to think less of him. He can neither "acknowledge his creatureliness" nor "admit his insecurity." Not only does he seek to "hide" these facts of his life but also "the dishonesty by which he sought to obscure these." [39] For instance, he will rarely tell others about his weaknesses or misdeeds even if they weigh heavily upon him. The searing memory of failures as a parent or failure in his line of work remains tightly locked within. Regretted instances of dishonesty and immorality prey upon his mind but are never discussed. Or if some mention is made of these, it is in a vague and general way that cloaks their real meaning.

The same is true of what he thinks about himself. Regardless of whether he has done what society expects and approves, he is likely to believe that he has not and yet conceal this belief from others. Where he sees himself inferior to those he admires or envies, he may even pretend superiority in order to ease the pain it causes him. In short, the more strongly he doubts his own worth as a human, the more vigorously he will deny it before the world. Such an attempt "to become what you are not" inevitably leads to "pretense" and "hypocrisy," born of a "compulsion to be something other, better and more ideal than what one is." [40]

The Cautious Manner

This guardedness can be seen not only in what he says, but in the manner in which he says it. He lacks the relaxed, "constant openness" of the Christian—a kind of "liberation" or "detachment" from the world.[41] It is as though each thought and utterance cannot be trusted until he asks himself: "How will this sound?" "What would happen if I said that?" "Can I trust telling him?" He hesitates, at times stammers or looks confused, and may seem anxious or embarrassed. There is a certain shallowness about his words and exclamations. They tend to be flat and stereotyped with little "vital self-expression" or spontaneity. When something more revealing does slip through, his feeling of alarm or discomfort usually evidences a "psychic underground." [42] He apologizes profusely, explains it away, or stiffly ignores it; but underlying guardedness is often betrayed by his stiff and repetitive tones, looks, or gestures. How honest he is with his thoughts is seldom unrelated to how safe and studied they sound.[43]

The more important the thought, of course, the more careful he is with it. Deeply held convictions are generally aired only in the company of those known to share them, especially if he values the esteem of such persons. He may expound an unpopular belief about free enterprise or the divinity of Christ in the presence of like-minded believers or unvalued skeptics, but not among the respected orthodox. Where such hypocrisy is in danger of being exposed, he becomes cautious about all possibly controversial utterances. Carried to an extreme, this may result in a person who fears even to question the established beliefs and values of his own social group. Whether a member of the great middle class or a free-thinking hippie, he learns to think twice about expressing each thought that comes naturally.

Over the years he may submerge his doubts and "believe

what he cannot believe." Wishing "to be rid of doubts once and for all," he may chose "blind acceptance" of the prevailing beliefs.[44] But he will continue to reveal his underlying sensitivity to such rebellious impulses by the way he reacts when others express them. Such a person becomes like the pious Job of the Prologue, expressionlessly intoning "Blessed be the name of the Lord" lest the distant plea of his wife to "curse God, and die" find its mark.[45]

Honest Versus Dishonest Expression

There is a difference, then, between the quality of expression found in the mature Christian and that possible in a life untouched by God's redeeming grace. The difference is in the "openness" and "ultimate honesty" of the mature Christian.[46] He is able to express his desires, feelings, thoughts, and doubts naturally and without fear. There is a refreshing frankness and spontaneity about the way he shows himself to others, even those he most desires to please. He can "forget" himself.[47] In direct contrast is the man lacking the Christian's freeing sense of security. This man is a prisoner of his own fears. He fears to feel anything deeply, whether anger, lust, love, or delight, lest he lose control of himself and forfeit the respect of the respectable. He dares not even admit his own doubts, for they seem to him traitorous and threatening. The brittle shell that remains, a monument to the "destruction of human self-hood," [48] requires for its maintenance every fleeting vitality he possesses.

III

Avoiding the Pitfalls of "Expression" Testing

There are a few empirical indicators that discriminate between persons generally disposed toward inhibition of thoughts and feelings and those able to express themselves freely. Yet care must be taken to select indicators that reflect more the freedom to express one's inner life than a driven necessity to exhibit oneself or rebel against authority. Many so-called "expression" tests or inventories in use today don't do the job, so one should be wary of accepting undocumented claims or impressive-sounding names.

Freud's Method and "Rule"

For sheer reliability there is probably no better method than clinical observation. Honest expression has long been recognized as the "fundamental technical rule" of therapeutic relationship as well as one of its major goals.[49] As a consequence, there are few areas of human behavior of greater concern to the clinician. Nor is it surprising that his training and experience usually make him particularly sensitive to the ways we have of hiding our important thoughts and feelings.

Among the clinician's most telling indicators are forgetting and blocking. As he leads the subject into touchy areas, he notes omissions and hesitations in the subject's train of thought. Yet what is related may be equally revealing. Evasive expression often makes use of clichés and stereotyped phrases or emphasizes the external and physical aspects of personally important events. In the give-and-take of conversation, how appropriate the subject's expressed feelings are also indicates his degree of openness. Aloof detachment, irritation, embarrassment, nervous laughter, and levity fitting neither the content of what is said nor the occasion are often seen as indicators of unexpressed feelings. But in the end it is the way the experienced clinician tempers, weighs, and synthesizes these factors over an extended period of time that gives the method of clinical observation its superior reliability.

A clinical technique that has found its way into objectively scored testing is free association. A list of words is read to or by a subject who is instructed to respond with the first word or words that occur to him. Some of the listed words have an emotionally neutral content, and some have sexual, aggressive, or other possibly threatening connotations. Responses can be scored for reaction time (latency), appropriateness of associated word (imaginativeness, oddness, literalness, etc.), number of associated words, and skin conductivity (GSR). Sentence completion tests are of a similar order. Again the object is to measure the discrepancy between the subject's response to emotionally neutral and to emotionally threatening material. Here the subject is asked to complete a list of sentences missing verbs or predicates. Scoring indicators like excessive length or abstrusive content can be used in addition to those mentioned above.

Picture Tests

Pictures are often as revealing of genuine expression as words or incomplete sentences. One group of experimenters[50] gave subjects a pile of sixty pictures to sort. The pictures varied in content, artistic style, and emotional value. The pictures were sorted into "liking," "no feeling," and "disliking" piles on the basis of immediate impression. Subjects were scored on the number of pictures sorted into the "no feeling" pile and on the number of hesitations observed. The test is designed especially for those who use words to cover up their lack of feeling, since neither the stimulus nor response requires verbalization.

Cartoons can be put to a similar use, as a study by Levine and Abelson[51] illustrates. Twenty selected *New Yorker* cartoons were rated on a seven-point scale for aggressiveness and sexual "disturbingness" by five clinically trained judges. Subjects sorted the cartoons into "like," "neutral," and "dislike" piles and then selected the five most liked and the five most disliked cartoons. An experimenter recorded the subject's laughs and smiles for each cartoon. On all three indexes of this "Mirth Response Test" clinically diagnosed disturbed and anxious subjects indicated significantly less liking for the more disturbing cartoons than did the normals. The authors interpret the difference between groups in terms of "mastering or coping with aroused anxiety."

The Rosenzweig Picture Frustration Test is a variation designed to measure the way a person characteristically expresses his anger. The subject is shown a series of cartoons depicting one person frustrating another. In each the frustrater is shown saying something (printed inside a "balloon"), and the subject is asked to fill in the blank balloon belonging to the victim with the first answer that comes to mind. In their version of this test Roberts and Jessor[52] used twenty-four cartoons. Half the cartoons depicted a frustrater of higher social status than the victim, and half depicted a frustrater of lower social status. Against each type of frustrater a subject's responses were scored for expression of direct hostility, scapegoated hostility, self-directed hostility, and lack of hostility.

Other kinds of pictured life situations can test how comfortably a person is able to express and control emotion. One of the most ingenious of these[53] is a set of eight pictures containing vague cues suggesting that the main character has lost control of himself or is in a dangerous situation. One pictures a rider on horseback possibly losing his balance; another pictures a woman on top of a water tower, etc. The subject is asked to rate five possible interpretations ranging from those affirming that the protagonist is firmly in control of himself to those asserting the likelihood that he has decidedly lost control. The authors reason, and present some empirical evidence to show, that persons who consistently see the pictured characters at either extreme are reacting to their own fear of losing control over inner disturbances.

Redesigning the TAT

The Thematic Apperception Test (TAT) is among the most widely used measures of expression. A skilled interpreter can usually spot the type of stories told about TAT pictures which betray distrust of feelings and impulses. But there is often a question of whether the more basic emotions attributed to TAT characters are those which the subject feels and cannot openly express himself or those which he can and does express. Testers agree only that emotion-laden stories from a subject who expresses little feeling in everyday life indicate marked inhibitation. Little can be learned from TAT responses that lack emotional color. In any event, it is usually necessary to have an independent measure of a subject's emotional strength or expression for comparison with his TAT stories.

A way out of this dilemma has been suggested by Murstein.[54] He proposes a method of interpretation that focuses on the fluctuations in strength of an emotion attributed to a story character as the TAT picture depicting this emotion becomes less and less veiled. For example, in a series of pictures where each picture shows more obvious hostility than the last, the open expresser would be expected to concoct a series of stories of increasing hostility. The subject who inhibits his hostility would either show no significant variation in the hostility content of his stories or, more likely, would show a rapid increase of hostility expression up to a point and then a marked decrease as the picture stimulus became more direct and threatening. As a theory of interpretation this proposal is quite elegant, but it may be years before we have enough empirical evidence to tell how well it works.

The Moving Light Revisited

Some experimental work has been reported with the auto-kinetic effect (a light that seems to move in a darkened room) which suggests a close relationship between tolerance for unrealistic experiences and the ability to express one's thoughts and feelings freely. Predicting that the subject who is free to relax and "be himself" is less inhibited in differing phases of his behavior, Temerlin[55] exposed two student groups of psychotherapy patients to the autokinetic effect. One group had been classified as extremely flexible and productive in free association, able to respond without hesitation and with appropriate feeling. Subjects in the other group had been diagnosed as extremely rigid and unproductive in free association, blocking, passive, and unable to come to terms with their resistances. The groups were matched for age, sex, intelligence, and socio-economic status.

Each subject was given fifty trials in the darkened room, reporting only the distance that the light seemed to move. The expressive subjects showed five times more variability of light movement than the inhibited subjects, with 80 per cent of the inhibited group scoring lower than the lowest subject in the expressive group. The author explains the result in terms of basic similarities between the free association and the autokinetic situation. Both, he claims, are highly unstructured. The subject is faced with a new and unfamiliar experience for which there is a minimum of instructions or guidelines. For one type of personality this elicits a defensive reaction that manifests inself in free-association blocking and autokinetic constrictedness. In a different type of personality neither of these occurs because lack of structure is not perceived as threatening.

A Footnote on the MMPI

Of all the questionnaires, inventories, and other paper-and-pencil tests claiming to measure self-expression there is probably only one that does it well: the Minnesota Multiphasic Personality Inventory (MMPI). This is partly because the MMPI is a complex instrument (ten basic scales, three corrective scales, and hundreds of special-use scales) and partly because it has been around for nearly thirty years and few of its limitations remain unknown. How accurately the MMPI can identify the essential characteristics of honest expression depends greatly upon the use to which it is put and the quality of interpretation. Many have come to grief from attempting a mechanical interpretation of test results. A high or low score on any one scale, or even a number of scales, tells the interpreter very little. It is the dynamic relationship between them in the light of what he already knows about the subject that makes it a valuable indicator of many personality traits, but perhaps especially those that affect the quality of a person's expression.

Too Many Projectives?

With the exception of the first and the last two measures, every empirical indicator described above is a type of projective test. Generally it is wise to employ measures of many types when attempting to identify a characteristic so subtle as honest expression. A search for such measures has proved disappointing except in the case of the three exceptions described. With the group of measures weighted so heavily on the projective side, it is of crucial importance to know how well-suited projectives are for identifying characteristics of honest expression. Two issues bear upon the type of answer that can be given.

Some eyebrows may be raised by the use of any projectives

for the purposes proposed by this chapter. Projectives, it is said, reveal what is felt, not what can be expressed. This is at least partially true. Most projectives are designed to elicit the expression of thoughts and feelings in a way that is perceived less dangerous or anxiety provoking by the subject, thus somewhat artificially. The word, picture, story, etc., employed as the projective stimulus appears to be "about" someone or something else or is of such a generalized nature that less risk is involved in identifying oneself with it. While projectives have been used primarily to identify the particular *type* of thoughts and feelings experienced by the subject, certain projective designs and interpretive techniques will also indicate the *extent* to which these thoughts and feelings are inhibited. The selection above has been made to include a number of the better projectives in this latter group.

Granting this, one may raise a further question regarding the marked emphasis upon aggressive and sexual content in the projective stimulus. Does not the mature Christian express a far broader range of thoughts and feelings? The answer, of course, is yes. Few projective designs have as yet reached beyond this concern to tap other areas of expression and inhibition, with the possible exception of those which deal broadly with the phenomenon of social desirability or general defensiveness. Yet there seems to be both theoretical and empirical justification for this emphasis. Not only have sexual and aggressive impulses and their derivatives been considered the root of most socially undesirable traits (and thus the prime targets of repressive tendencies), but the consistent empirical finding across a broad range of experimental situations has been that sexually and aggressively connoted words and pictures are among the first to be defended against.

Again, this does not put to rest all uneasiness about the package of empirical indicators discussed in this chapter, nor should it. There is a decided need for more and better measures of honest expression, even among the projectives. Yet with these limitations in view, there is no reason to doubt that the empirical indicators at hand can be of significant value in discriminating the honest expresser from his less secure neighbor.

IV

At the Halfway Mark

We turn now from noting how the mature Christian (and his opposite) perceives and responds to his own inner promptings, to how the world of people and events affects his behavior. What each man sees of the world and the way he responds to it are not unrelated to what he sees and responds to in himself. Common to both "subjective" and "objective" perspectives on a man's life style is the degree to which it is founded upon a freeing sense of security. A glance at the diagram on page 23 will make more sense now and should be consulted if you are having difficulty putting the scheme of this book together. It should be apparent how each of these last two chapters (and the next two chapters) is an expanded look at a particular area of the "basic" Chapter II.

The theological focus of the next chapter is on revelation. If it never occurred to you that the doctrine of revelation says much about the mature Christian and how he may be empirically identified, you may learn something.

NOTES

1. I Cor. 12:12-31.
2. Luther, *Galatians 1-4*, p. 70; Bonhoeffer, *Life Together*, pp. 112-13.
3. Calvin, *Institutes*, i.14, 1.
4. *Ibid.*, ii.8, 22; cf. ii.8, 35, also i.2, 2.
5. *Ibid.*, iii.7, 10.
6. Søren Kierkegaard, *Sickness unto Death* (in *Fear and Trembling and the Sickness unto Death*), pp. 154, 167, 182, 213; cf. Bultmann, *Essays*, p. 306; Bonhoeffer, *Ethics*, p. 22; Reinhold Niebuhr, *Destiny*, p. 123.
7. Bultmann, *Essays*, p. 306; cf. Martin Luther, "Preface to the Book of Psalms," *The Spirit of the Protestant Reformation*, ed. and trans. Bertram Lee Woolf ("The Reformation Writings of Martin Luther," Vol. II; London: Lutterworth, 1956), pp. 268-70; Calvin, *Institutes*, ii.2, 1; Kierkegaard, *For Self-examination*, p. 33; Bonhoeffer, *Letters and Papers*, p. 219; *Cost of Discipleship*, pp. 154-55.
8. Bultmann, *Essays*, p. 150; Tillich, *Systematic Theology*, III, 240.
9. Barth, IV/2, 612-13; Bultmann, *Essays*, pp. 300, 307-8.
10. Calvin, *Institutes*, iii.20, 6; cf. Tillich, *Dynamics of Faith*, p. 46; Bonhoeffer, *Ethics*, p. 114 n., Barth, III/4, 91.
11. Calvin, *Institutes*, iii.8, 9; also ii.16, 11-12; Luther, *Galatians 1-4*, p. 55.
12. Mark 14:33-35.
13. Luther, "Psalms," pp. 268-70; cf. Tillich, *Systematic Theology*, III, 240; Reinhold Niebuhr, *Destiny*, p. 210; Bonhoeffer, *Ethics*, p. 250; Luther, *Galatians 1-4*, pp. 55, 175-76.
14. Mark 15:34.
15. Tillich, *Systematic Theology*, III, 191; cf. Bonhoeffer, *Letters and Papers*, pp. 87-88; Luther, *Galatians 1-4*, pp. 340-42; Calvin, *Institutes*, iii.2, 18; Kierkegaard, *For Self-examination*, pp. 37-38.
16. Bonhoeffer, *Letters and Papers*, p. 105.
17. Luther, "Psalms" pp. 268-70; cf. *Galatians 1-4*, pp. 70, 230; Kierkegaard, *For Self-examination*, p. 50; Calvin, *Institutes*, iii.3, 3; Bonhoeffer, *Life Together*, p. 112; Barth III/2, 254; Reinhold Niebuhr, *Interpretation*, p. 195; Bultmann, *Essays*, p. 150.
18. Bonhoeffer, *Ethics*, p. 114n.; cf. Kierkegaard, *Postscript*, p. 485; Bonhoeffer, *Cost of Discipleship*, p. 57; H. Richard Niebuhr, *Radical Monotheism and Western Culture* (New York: Harper, 1957), pp. 51-53.
19. II Cor. 11:16–12:13.
20. II Sam. 6:16.
21. Kierkegaard, *Fear and Trembling*, pp. 49-51; cf. Bonhoeffer, *Letters and Papers*, pp. 123-24; Barth, III/4, 672; Reinhold Niebuhr, *Interpretation*, p. 149.
22. Barth, IV/3(1), 457 n.; Tillich, *Shaking of the Foundations*, p. 42; Luther, "Psalms," pp. 255-70; Kierkegaard, *Postscript*, pp. 521-22; Bultmann, *Essays*, pp. 323-24.
23. Mark 11:15-19.

24. Bonhoeffer, *Letters and Papers*, p. 175; Bultmann, *Essays*, pp. 294-95; Kierkegaard, *Postscript*, p. 317; Schleiermacher, *Christian Faith*, p. 675.

25. Bonhoeffer, *Ethics*, pp. 13, 114, 250; *Letters and Papers*, p. 113; Barth III/4, 348.

26. Reinhold Niebuhr, *Destiny*, pp. 91, 201 n.; Bonhoeffer, *Ethics*, pp. 175, 234; Calvin, *Institutes*, iii.3, 12; H. Richard Niebuhr, *Christ and Culture* (New York: Harper, 1951), p. 212.

27. Ruth 1:15-18; I Sam. 20:17.

28. Kierkegaard, *Postscript*, p. 317; Bultmann, *Essays*, p. 306; Barth, III/2, 254; Reinhold Niebuhr, *Destiny*, pp. 91-92.

29. Kierkegaard, *Postscript*, pp. 317, 521-22; Bonhoeffer, *Letters and Papers*, pp. 189-90.

30. Jer. 20:13-14.

31. Bultmann, *Essays*, pp. 115, 294-95, 306, 314; Reinhold Niebuhr, *Nature*, p. 256; *Destiny*, p. 123; Tillich, *Systematic Theology*, III, 211.

32. Reinhold Niebuhr, *Destiny*, p. 201 n.; cf. Bultmann, *Essays*, p. 148; Tillich, *Systematic Theology*, III, 240; Bonhoeffer, *Cost of Discipleship*, p. 149; Calvin, *Institutes*, iii.8, 9.

33. Bonhoeffer, *Letters, and Papers*, pp. 191-92.

34. Barth, III/4, 98; cf. Bonhoeffer, *Letters and Papers*, pp. 123-24; *Cost of Discipleship*, p. 57; Bultmann, *Kerygma and Myth*, pp. 3-4; Tillich, *Protestant Era*, p. 133.

35. Calvin, *Institutes*, iii.8, 9.

36. Tillich, *Systematic Theology*, III, 240; cf. Tillich, *Protestant Era*, p. 133; Bonhoeffer, *Ethics*, p. 19; Luther, *Galatians 5-6*, p. 71; Bultmann, *Essays*, p. 170; *Kerygma and Myth*, p. 211.

37. Bultmann, *Essays*, p. 150; cf. Bultmann, *Christ and Mythology*, p. 41; Reinhold Niebuhr, *Nature*, pp. 29-30.

38. Bonhoeffer, *Life Together*, p. 111; *Ethics*, p. 19; Bultmann, *Essays*, pp. 294-95, 314; Barth III/4, 98.

39. Bultmann, *Essays*, p. 314; Reinhold Niebuhr, *Nature*, pp. 137-38, 150, 256; cf. Bonhoeffer, *Life Together*, pp. 112-13; Tillich, *Systematic Theology*, III, 191; H. Richard Niebuhr, *Revelation*, p. 114.

40. Bonhoeffer, *Ethics*, p. 19; *Cost of Discipleship*, p. 57; cf. Reinhold Niebuhr, *Interpretation*, p. 83; Tillich, *Protestant Era*, p. 133; Bultmann, *Essays*, pp. 294-96.

41. Bultmann, *Essays*, p. 300; *Kerygma and Myth*, p. 20.

42. Barth, III/2, 254; Tillich, *Systematic Theology*, III, 240; *Protestant Era*, p. 133.

43. Kierkegaard, *Postscript*, pp. 68 n., 216; Bultmann, *Essays*, pp. 300, 307-8; Bonhoeffer, *Cost of Discipleship*, p. 57.

44. Tillich, *Shaking of the Foundations*, p. 97; Kierkegaard, *Postscript*, p. 44; Bultmann, *Kerygma and Myth*, pp. 3-4; cf. Barth, III/2, 254; Bultmann, *Essays*, p. 37; Tillich, *Protestant Era*, pp. x-xi; *Systematic Theology*, III, 228, 240; Bonhoeffer, *Letters and Papers*, p. 104; Calvin, *Institutes*, iii.2, 18; Kierkegaard, *Training in Christianity*, p. 83.

45. Job 1:20-21; 2:9-10.

46. Bultmann, *Essays*, p. 306; Bonhoeffer, *Letters and Papers*, p. 219.

47. Reinhold Niebuhr, *Destiny*, p. 123.

48. *Ibid.*, p. 99.

49. Sigmund Freud, *A General Introduction to Psychoanalysis* (New York: Washington Square Press, 1960), p. 298.

50. Riley W. Gardner, "Cognitive Control," pp. 1-185.

51. Jacob Levine and Robert Abelson, "Humor as a Disturbing Stimulus," *Journal of General Psychology*, LX (1959), 191-200.

52. Alan H. Roberts and Richard Jessor, "Authoritarianism, Punitiveness, and Perceived Social Status," *Journal of Abnormal and Social Psychology*, LVI (1958), 311-14.

53. Seymour Fisher and Rhoda L. Fisher, "The Effects of Personal Insecurity on Reactions to Unfamiliar Music," *Journal of Social Psychology*, XXXIV (1951), 265-73.

54. Bernard I. Murstein, *Theory and Research in Projective Techniques (Emphasizing the TAT)* (New York: Wiley, 1963), pp. 69-83.

55. Maurice K. Temerlin, "One Determinant of the Capacity to Free-associate in Psychotherapy," *Journal of Abnormal and Social Psychology*, LIII (1956), 16-18.

─────────── *chapter V* ───────────

SEEING WHAT IS THERE

I

Where Accurate Perception Fits with the Christian Life

Living in the world as a Christian means knowing what is going on in the world. With minor exceptions, perhaps, human existence limits our knowledge of the world to that which we see, hear, touch, smell, and taste. The Christian perceives reality not by transcending the senses, but by allowing them to function freely. He does not jeopardize his view of the world by requiring that his senses also protect shaky feelings of security. Christian perception is accurate perception, no matter how strong the storm outside or the feelings within.

Most world religions, Christianity included, seek to know the nature and will of a Supreme Being. The God of the Christian and Jew is believed to reveal himself primarily through what he has created, sustained, and redeemed. Such revelation is indirect, or "contingent," for what is known about God must be inferred from the worldly evidences of nature and history. God's "hand" is seen in both the ordinary and the extraordinary, but never his face.

The Sharper Eye

Christianity claims to point to the ultimate expression of worldly revelation in Jesus Christ. Here the divine nature and will of God are said to be revealed in a simple human life plus the events that issue from his death and resurrection. Yet so ordinary appearing are most of these events, both past and present, that the Christian church finds it necessary in every age to explain why some persons see God at work in them while others do not. Most explanations claim that God has given the Christian eyes to see—a certain gift, power, grace, or faith not possessed by those outside the church. Those who fail to see, he has blinded or allowed Satan to blind, or they have fallen into blindness because of their sinfulness. Every formulation bristles with problems, yet they hold in common the assumption that the Christian is able to perceive a good deal more of the world through which God reveals himself than can his non-Christian brother.

Early Protestant understanding of revelation placed a special emphasis upon accurate perception. God's Word was not to be confused with man's word. For the reformers this meant shifting the focus of attention from the fixed dogma of the church to the unchanging Word of God in its ever changing finite expressions. Since this Word was in no way contained by human institutions, knowledge, or understanding, the reformers saw it most clearly reflected in that portion of scripture which turned the Christian's eyes toward God's saving actions in the world.

The senses have a special importance to the reformers because they are the means by which the saving Word is appropriated. Correct perception not only informs the mind but also nourishes the soul. Knowledge of God and saving grace are one and the same; both come by Jesus Christ and are received through the senses. While the medieval Christian had little religious interest in the acuity of his senses, believing his salvation rested mainly upon the ministrations of his church and the works he performed, the early Protestant saw his justification based squarely on the sense-mediated reception of such divine knowledge.

Sin and the Senses

It is little wonder, then, that Protestant theologians have been concerned with the quality of perception. Where the senses distort reality, where they convey false impressions of the world in which God reveals himself for man's salvation, the power of sin prevails. In fact, the greater the hold of sin on a man's heart, the more he is deceived by his senses. Luther believed that the devil's "bewitchment of the senses" was both a cause and a result of "bewitchment of the spirit." [1] Calvin recognized that sin affected the accuracy of the senses mainly in those areas of life which threaten one's basis of security. In the arts and sciences, argued Calvin, the unbeliever is often as clear-sighted and perceptive as the Christian; but in matters of spiritual importance touching feelings of fear or pride, the unbeliever protects himself by perceiving things that do not exist and misperceiving those that do.[2] Recent Protestant thought has elaborated this view with the aid of depth psychology, but there has been little reason to challenge the reformers' basic insight that the corruption of the heart and the corruption of the senses go hand in hand.

Contemporary theology has tended to emphasize the pastoral implications of this view. Not only is accurate perception the means and sign of spiritual strength, it is also the condition of Christian service. To minister in the name of Christ requires an acute sensitivity to the needs of others.

Where this is lacking, gross errors of judgment that block or misdirect the best human efforts inevitably occur. Protestant theologians are speaking today of a "ministry of listening." The Christian listens not only to hear God's Word in a complex and fragmented world, but to respond to his Word in a way that answers the deepest needs of his fellowman. To be unable to perceive these needs, needs through which God both speaks and is served, is seen to severely limit the ministry of service demanded of every Christian.

Life Together

Yet at the root of Christian life is still another ground for perceptual accuracy. As much Protestant theology is currently stressing, the Christian lives in community with others. At the interpersonal level this means that the strength and quality of human relationships are dependent upon social sensitivity. Without a sensitive awareness of another's life, Christian love is impossible. The family and the church are often given as examples of human institutions having possibilities for spiritual nourishment only as great as the possibilities for significant communication between their members.

Even at a level of social organization where face-to-face encounter is less frequent (as in large political and industrial structures), effectiveness of communication can mean the difference between enrichment and corrosion of the Christian life. Complex human organization often requires a sharper eye for affairs of human importance than do simple and direct personal relationships. In either case, however, it is plain that mature Christian life is not achieved in solitude. The body of Christ has many members who nourish one another as they are nourished. However simple or complex the tie between them, it can be no better than the social sensitivity that supports it.

All in all, it would be difficult to point to a single doctrine emphasized in Protestant thought that does not presuppose accurate perception. There is no place in Christian theology for a distorted view of reality. In the section to follow, some of the more important areas of perceptual activity implied by Protestant thought will be described as they are found in life situations.

II

"Open to the Life of the World" [3]

To see the world as it is a person must be in full command of his senses. By means of them the Christian receives a true picture of the world in which he lives. He sees, hears, smells, tastes, and feels "everything as it—objectively, really . . . is." [4] This does not mean that he perceives everything that goes on around him, as might a trained spy or detective. He may not have especially keen senses. Rather, he is distinguished by the ability to perceive the things that have immediate relevance for him as adequately as he is able to perceive anything else. What he sees does not affect how well he sees. He "sees in the given situation what is necessary." [5]

The Christian approaches life with an "openness" to the myriad of experiences it affords.[6] Like everyone else, he forms opinions and develops beliefs about the things he perceives. Some of these judgments about the world are no more complex than being aware that a particular object exists or an event is occurring. Able to "open all organs to the influence of all impressions," he may take them all in with hardly a thought.[7] But when it happens that he must act or reflect on the basis of what he has noticed, he finds the world much as he had imagined it. He has been given an "ear to hear and the mind to understand." [8]

For Example

Let us say the mature Christian buys a car. Suppose it is his first new car and he has a great deal invested in it, financially and emotionally. Whether he understands cars mechanically or not, he expects a certain quality of performance from this car, based upon past experience with the same make, manufacturer's claims, consumer testing organizations, and the like. After the first week of driving he is pleased with the car and feels he has made an excellent choice. Its performance matches his expectations.

Then the trouble begins. At first it is just a rattle, perhaps something to be expected. Then there is a new sound, smell, or vibration nearly every time he drives it. He seeks expert advice. His dealer discounts the difficulties and makes a few adjustments. A garage mechanic across town says it's a lemon and advises him to sell immediately. How does the Christian respond?

If he decides not to sell, the Christian's view of the car continues to reflect what actually happens each time he drives it—just as it would if the car were not his own. While some unhappy new owners fail to notice worrisome signs of trouble after a while and convince themselves accordingly, the Christian is not deceived. He lives within, not "beyond," his "perceptive faculties." [9] Without denying his initial hopes and expectations, he continues to adjust them to the way his car is performing. Nor will he begin hearing noises that are not there, even if he decides to sell the car. Regardless of how much he regrets what has happened or what he does about it, he neither overestimates nor underestimates the perceptible mechanical difficulties. In other words, his picture of "visible and audible and perceptible" reality is constantly—often unknowingly—being checked against the actual situation through basic sense perceptions. [10] The Christian may not possess the trained ear or the technical judgment of the experienced mechanic, but what he has he uses.[11]

Of course, the heightened perception enabled by Christian maturity is never an adequate substitute for technical knowledge and skill. But this is not to say that Christian maturity does not affect the quality of this technical proficiency. When the experienced garage mechanic listens to an engine, for instance, he hears only what he is prepared to hear. Training and experience prepare him to accurately identify a greater range of potential trouble spots, but the pressure of time, irritation at the owner, hurt pride, or the chance to make extra money *can* lead him to "disregard . . . some of the obvious evidences" and introduce error into his "calculations." [12] Christian maturity provides the basic security to withstand the inner temptations which lead even qualified technicians to make premature judgments on the basis of insufficient evidence.

This is as true in the spotless research laboratory as in the greasy mechanic's pit. When a scientist devotes months or years of his life in the hope of finding a predicted result, he is as vulnerable to perceptual distortion as he is when he buys a new car. As a researcher the Christian fails to notice disconfirming evidence no more often than that which accords with his hopes and expectations. Whatever may pose a threat to him is perceived as readily as is an object of desire. He has the ability to see "things as they are" with "scientific objectivity." [13]

Caleb and the Two Vietnams

Public affairs provide another arena for the perceptive abilities of the mature Christian. The undeclared war in Vietnam offers an example of a frustrating military and political situation about which men of superior training and good intentions often disagree, even in the analysis of a particular local military or political situation. One is reminded of Caleb, whom Moses commissioned "to spy out the land of Canaan." [14] Caleb observed everything his companions did. He saw the number of the Canaanites and the strength of their cities, as well as the richness of their land. He may even have seen an oversized warrior or two. But unlike his companions, the prospect that he might soon meet them in battle did not make them appear any larger or more numerous than they actually were.

The modern counterpart to this ancient tale was reported to have occurred in Washington a few years ago. Two Vietnam observers, obviously of different persuasions, were asked to brief President Kennedy on the logistics of the conflict. When they had finished, the puzzled Commander-in-Chief asked, "Are you gentlemen sure you visited the same country?" [15] Certainly wars are not won nor conflicts settled on the basis of accurate strategic observation alone, but when qualified military and civilian observers disagree so widely on matters of comparative troop strengths and casualty lists, one need look little further than poor perceptual judgment. If the Christian lacks sufficient evidence on which to base a reliable estimate, he reports this. He does not kid himself into believing that he sees better than he does.[16]

Social issues of the day afford another test of perceptual abilities. We are often tempted to conclude that liberals and conservatives disagree basically on desired ends of social policy, or at least on the best means of gaining a common end. But when without intention loyal party members become strangely blind to the same graft and bossism they so effortlessly perceive in the opposing party organization, something more elemental is occurring. The Christian may have a moral responsibility to take a particular stand on a social issue. But if he is acting as a mature Christian, and not merely as a moral Christian, he will give himself to "attentive observation of the given facts" that support both sides of the issue.[17]

Eyewitness observation is perhaps the most direct way of ascertaining this kind of information. The mature Christian checking slum properties for housing code violations by landlords notices evidence of tenant neglect and damage too. As a witness to a racial incident, he does not allow his sympathies for the underdog to distort what he sees, hears, or remembers. Yet the Christian is equally open to other sources of information. What he understands at first reading of a news story describing an incident may be less than the next man absorbs, but that which escapes his eye favors one side of the controversy no more than the other.

It is basically the same for all other communication media. He may notice or retain very little of what jumps out at him from newspapers, magazines, radio, or television. When it is a matter of preference, he may attend more closely to what interests him and even avoid articles, books, and programs that do not reflect his personal views. But given a purpose for informing himself on a particular topic, he seldom confuses his inward leanings with what lies before his eyes.

Social Sensitivity

The mature Christian will also be sensitive to that which goes on in the lives of persons around him. He is in "open perception of the other." [18] This is especially true when to perceive correctly is to perceive unwelcome signs.[19] He is like Ahab, who inquired of the prophet Micaiah about the probable success of a military venture. Despite his personal dislike for Micaiah for divining past signs of misfortune, he was able to perceive behind Micaiah's more hopeful words the prophet's ominous vision of "all Israel scattered upon the mountains." [20] Sensing what another thinks is not mind reading. It has more to do with noticing how the person speaks and acts in response to others. It is one of the most complex social skills known to man and as such is highly vulnerable to whatever is going on within the perceiver. Both skill and native ability are needed. But the Christian observer who possesses these gifts stands a better chance of perceiving the other's thoughts than perceiving the shadow of his own.[21]

The ability to fathom attitudes and feelings of others is just as important. The Christian experiences little difficulty "putting himself in the other man's place."[22] Regardless of personal differences, whether of background, attitude, belief, or friendship, he is able to sense how the other feels.[23] Again, skill and experience may determine how effectively he can use this advantage. But it is the Christian's undefended openness toward those with whom he comes in personal contact that allows him to share, and thus to experience for himself, the "cares, the needs, the joys" of friend and stranger alike.[24]

Jesus

This is not always to "rejoice with those who rejoice" and "weep with those who weep,"[25] but to be able to. Perhaps no other characteristic of the mature Christian life reminds us as much of Jesus. So remarkable was his sensitivity toward people, that in nearly every recorded personal encounter Jesus is described as perceptively aware of the other's thoughts and feelings, even if the person himself might lack such awareness.

Yet it is Jesus' sensitivity to the often conflicting feelings of persons that best qualifies him as an illustration of accurate perception. He saw in Martha's "anxious and troubled" manner the struggle between the desire to open herself to him and the desire to keep her distance.[26] Behind the words and "sorrowful" response of the rich young man, Jesus became aware of a deep conflict between two desires.[27] And he sensed within the woman anointing his feet the turning of a desperate battle that no other guest perceived.[28] To so open oneself to the experience of the world and to the lives of others is what is meant by accurate perception.

Blind to the World

There is also the kind of person who colors reality to suit his own wishes or expectations. Although his senses may be keen, he often fails to notice what is really there. His senses are "corrupt" and his mind "blinded."[29] This is especially true when he feels himself to be insecure and the world to be "hostile and harmful."[30] The picture of the world such a person carries around in his head is likely to differ in few respects from that of the mature Christian. He may know every street and park in his city, be able to render a striking likeness of his twelve-year-old son in oils, and be able to accurately describe a complex business transaction. At most points his beliefs about the world are "acute and clearsighted."[31] The difference lies in the reliability of his views. Where the mature Christian finds it easy and natural to check his views against reality by means of sense perception, this man does not. In those areas of his life where the stakes are high and his emotional investment deep, he may slip mooring and drift off into a world of his own. He lacks "full awareness of reality."[32]

Perceiving the Unreal

Fantasy is not a sign of weakness. It is part of our child-like nature that we carry into adulthood and is the basis for many of our creative and imaginative abilities in later years. Fantasy expresses the unfulfilled hopes of life. Whether for the purpose of relieving our frustrations, delighting our sensibilities, or projecting realistic solutions, fantasy is a prized human possession. But fantasy confused with reality is not. The mature Christian knows when he is engaging in fantasy and when he is being realistic. Further, he has the ability to snap out of his world of fantasy at the intrusion of reality, as a dreamer awakes to the harsh ring of his alarm clock. The man lacking Christian maturity is still like a child in this respect. Instead of using fantasy, he is controlled by it, driven to the "construction of imaginary worlds." [33]

In extreme form he may perceive things that aren't there; "a man supposes he is seeing something that he really does not see, or hearing a voice . . . that he really does not hear." [34] People who hear voices and experience hallucinations are rearranging the outer world to suit their inner needs. Some are less than convinced by these perceptual tricks. They will tell you that they actually saw or heard certain unusual things but know that it couldn't be so. Others have lost all contact with reality in one area and become convinced that they have perceived something real. Under particular stress, they are "carried away by their own impressions." [35] Mass sightings of UFOs suggest that false perception and consequent belief can occur just as well outside mental institutions.

In the last analysis we see what we want to see. What we "cannot bear to see," we don't. [36] The Christian who can return from fantasy at a slight prompting from the world of reality indicates the priority of his desires. The man who cannot has somewhere along the line turned his back on the world and chosen to retreat into one of his own making, a world he wants to see and believe in. [37]

Misperceiving the Real

A more common area of fantasy's domain is the misperception of things that exist. Something is seen but not correctly.[38] For example, it is not unusual for two capable adults whose only major difference is party affiliation to arrive at entirely different head counts at a political rally. Both would like to see a certain number turnout, and so within the limits of their own credibility, they do.

The same thing is true of many social and ideological differences. For instance, superpatriots are by and large honest people. They would willingly deceive neither themselves nor others. Most superpatriots intend only to awaken their country to the deception and guile of an enemy. Yet their sworn claims of Communist activities at home are so obviously at variance with reality that we at once impune their honesty. What they do may have morally reprehensible (and commendable) features, but their actions are probably better understood as the results of unknowing misperception. A few Communists become more Communists, a slight leftist leaning becomes a strong leftist leaning, and so it goes. It is the "pathology of the man of sin" that "reality discloses itself to him in an image which is defaced, distorted, and corrupted." [39]

It matters little whether misperception occurs at first sight or later, since perception is a continuous process of testing reality which has gone awry in the man who lacks Christian maturity. A particular belief or ideology often becomes a refuge for such a man. It offers him a loyalty to something other than reality and thereby becomes for him a refuge from reality. He clings to it "when human perception is (often just from laziness) at an end." [40] Communism, capitalism, vegetarianism, Protestantism, can all be used as means of withdrawing from the world. Such isms often claim the sanctity of private judgments while ignoring the demands of perceptual honesty.

Perception or Judgment?

Yet it is obvious that poor judgment to a large extent involves poor perception. We misjudge because of a "distortion of our perception and thinking." [41] A distinction can be made between the perception of fact and the interpretation or judgment of fact, but it is often a misleading distinction. Were it possible to perceive the facts of a situation correctly but to interpret them wrongly, misperception would still be involved. Misperception lies at the root of all mistaken judgment, opinion, conviction, ideology, belief, and interpretation. A person's inner picture of the world that does not correspond to outer reality points to a long-standing breakdown of perceptive faculties, a cumulative error in assessing what is true and what is not true about the perceptible world. In the same way that the "jaundiced see everything as yellow," so "his sight is prejudiced more and more" until he "at last believes it." [42]

The mature Christian may hold an inaccurate world view and a mistaken judgment because of it, but he will not hold it long. Sooner or later he finds himself challenged by what he sees and hears.[43] The "challenge" is not an occasion for retreat into a more familiar and comfortable world, but a red flag indicating the need for a closer look at reality.[44] Discrepant facts catch his attention, bidding him to "observe . . . weigh up, assess and decide" how well they fit his picture of the world.[45]

Then begins the intricate process of realigning *his* world with *the* world. Where Christian maturity is lacking, this ongoing process of monitoring reality and correcting for error of belief breaks down. The sheer complexity of this process makes it highly vulnerable to feelings of insecurity.

In the person who inwardly desires to see a safe world more than a real world, the consequences of misperception reach even to the heart of his beliefs about the world. When a man "comes to fear the great, primary and central truth . . . he necessarily comes to fear the little, secondary, peripheral truths and . . . must try to translate and transform them into untruths." [46]

Social Blindness

Nowhere is this more evident than in the world of social relationships. The man who does not possess the freeing inner security of the mature Christian lives in a distorted society of his own making. Those who care for him are often believed to be against him, or at least to have ulterior motives for their concern. He may perceive accurately enough his wife's irritation or even indifference toward him on occasions, but not her warmth on other occasions. Yet with his secretary, his mother, or his son, affection may be all he perceives. Since he has an inner need to see people in terms of black and white, the intricate balance of feelings that pervades most human relationships becomes "imperceptible." [47] For this reason his homelife is often torn by unfounded accusations and groundless suspicious. What he may inwardly suspect or hope about himself he often believes about others, having lost the ability to correct his impressions by unclouded perception. He will "impute to all other selves the same interest in the self." [48]

Prejudice is the extension into the community of this crippled faculty. Such a person is invariably the first to see the weaknesses and failings of minority groups and their members, but he "does not notice" their virtues and accomplishments.[49] As the word implies, prejudice is the process of arriving at a conclusion unsupported by perceivable facts. The prejudiced person sees more clearly the group stereotype in his head than the person before his eyes.[50] After he shakes hands with a Negro, his hand feels dirty because he believes Negroes are dirty. He suspects that he was short-changed at Goldberg's Department Store because he is convinced that Jews will take advantage of people that way. Yet prejudice is as much a product of misperception as misperception is a result of prejudice. With all but the most sheltered individual, countless opportunities arise over the years to check feelings about groups against actual group members. The existence of prejudice itself is often evidence of a long history of misperception.

Seeing Jesus

Undoubtedly one of the things that has made the story of Jesus so fascinating to Western man is the striking paradox it poses in perceptual abilities. Jesus is the model par excellence of perceptual sensitivity, and those who opposed him, the model of prejudice. In most recorded instances it seems to be the combination of threat and the unexpected to which the perceptual accuracy—and consequent judgment —of his antagonists succumbed. Because he broke the expected pattern of piety and threatened a way of life, it became virtually impossible for many people to perceive Jesus as he was.[51] He was rejected at Nazareth by those whose knowledge of him as a child precluded knowledge of him as a man, even though he stood before them in full view and hearing.[52]

For this reason the Pharisees also took offense at him and consequently failed to perceive that which they of all people were best qualified to identify by virtue of their training and commitment.[53] The tragedy of the Pharisee was not that he willfully and knowledgeably opposed Jesus, but that he was inwardly so committed to his own view of the world that he failed to perceive the world as it was.

Like the Pharisee, the person lacking accurate perception will see only what he can afford to see; and that which goes against either his expectations or desires he will distort or else not notice.

The Nub of the Differences

As this contrast between Jesus and the Pharisees implies, the important difference between Christian perception and its absence does not lie so much in *how* a person views the world as *what* he sees of it. The mature Christian isn't primarily someone who sees things in a certain way. He doesn't see the world as beautiful or ugly, as God's handiwork or the devil's kingdom. He simply sees *more* of the world than most people. He can do this because of his "radical openness" to everything.[54] He can "listen freely to what goes against him"[55] and is not ruled by fears or rigid expectations of what lies beyond him.[56] "At every moment" he is able to "discover the improbable."[57] And so when he meets the new and unusual, he acknowledges its presence, often without really having to think about it. This is as true of his long-standing beliefs and convictions about the world as it is of his momentary perceptions, since he does not labor under the burden of years of cumulative misperceptions which have shaped his view of reality.

On the other hand, without the freeing sense of security known to the mature Christian a person's perception is jaded. His "corporeal senses" are affected "at every point."[58] They are often used in defense against the intrusion of the world. This means that his perception may be highly accurate one minute and mistaken the next, acute in one area and distorted in another. He is especially vulnerable at those points where he feels himself threatened and will often retreat into fantasy rather than risk acknowledging that he is not "able to stand" reality.[59] He shares only one thing with his mature Christian brother: he sees what he wants to see. But what he wants to see is a world that promises the sense of security he lacks within himself. He "fails to be addressed" by reality and finds reason for his "not hearing . . . in a not wanting to hear." [60]

III

Measuring Perception

Many of these same perceptual abilities and distortions have been the subject of intense empirical investigation in recent years. Experimental work has generally been concerned with two areas of perceived reality. The first has to do with a person's ability to perceive correctly various objects, representations of objects, or symbols. The second has to do directly with the perception of other persons.

Tachistoscopic Perception

The most widely used measures of perceptual accuracy of the first type are the tachistoscopic recognition tasks. The tachistoscope resembles a slide projector and is capable of projecting words, symbols, pictures, etc., on a screen or viewer in a number of ways that make correct recognition difficult. The subject is asked to identify the stimulus projected on the screen and is scored on the accuracy of his identification.

Methods of projection vary. Perhaps the most common method is simply to flash something on the screen at a very fast shutter speed. The number of exposures or "flashes" it takes for the subject to correctly guess the stimulus is scored. In some testing situations the shutter speed remains constant, and in others it gets progressively slower. Another method varies the amount of illumination. With shutter speed held constant, illumination is gradually increased until the subject makes the correct identification. The amount of illumination needed by the subject to see the projected stimulus is scored. Still a different method of projection holds shutter speed and illumination constant but gradually sharpens the focus of the projected figure until a correct identification is made.

The idea behind each of these methods is not to test a person's keenness of eyesight or his reading speed, but to compare his performance with different kinds of stimuli. A widely used comparison is between emotionally laden words ("love," "hate," "mother," etc.) and emotionally neutral words ("loud," "have," "matter," etc.) of similar form and frequency of use. Another common stimulus comparison is between expected and unexpected words, especially those matched for emotional tone, structural characteristics, and frequency of use. Pictures or symbols having established differences in anxiety-arousing properties are sometimes used. Perhaps the most intriguing comparison of all is between two words, symbols, or pictures having no intrinsic emotional meaning to the subject. One of the pair acquires emotional meaning, however, by becoming associated in his mind with a humiliating failure, a threat, or a sexually embarrassing situation (all experimentally contrived) minutes before the tachistoscopic test.

Nearly every subject, of course, perceives the emotionally neutral stimuli sooner and more accurately than the emotionally laden stimuli. But some subjects consistently record very small differences between the two types of stimuli, and some subjects record extremely large differences. What can account for this? In light of what has been said earlier in this chapter, it seems reasonable to suppose that the deciding factor is the freeing sense of security which allows the better perceiver to see what is before him regardless of how he feels about it. Unfortunately there seems to be no body of experimental work at present to indicate how correct this assumption may be. Tachistoscopic misperception has been linked with claimed indicators of repression,[61] but there is a lack of hard evidence to suggest that repression always indicates insecurity. About all that can be said at this point is that both theology and clinical experience affirm the assumed connection between perception and sense of security.

But Is This the Christian's "Accurate Perception"?

Perhaps the more important question to consider at present is whether the tachistoscopic recognition task is an adequate measure of accurate perception. The major characteristic of accurate perception as previously described is its unbiased nature, the receiving of a true picture of the world despite personal desires, threat, novelty, ambiguity, and other factors having immediate relevance to the perceiver. This implies more than identifying simple projected stimili. It implies more than one observation, or one series of observations, at a particular time. In the fullest sense accurate perception embraces the entire process by which a person becomes aware of the world around him and comes to hold certain beliefs about the nature of reality on the basis of it.

The question is then whether the type of tachistoscopic techniques used in recent experimental work is an *essential instance* of the way in which the system of perceptual processes work. Two lines of evidence suggest that this is in fact the case.

From what is known about how we see (hear, feel, etc.) things, it appears that perception resembles a scanning process not too unlike high-speed tachistoscopic exposure.

Evidently, we don't see something all at once but in bits and pieces. And these bits and pieces only make sense to us because we are half expecting to see them or guessing that we might see them. Our past experience provides a kind of frame of reference for these expectancies, and our inner desire to see what is before our eyes sets in motion a process something like hunting for pieces of a half-finished jigsaw puzzle. Without either the half-finished puzzle or the desire to complete the picture, perception is impossible or at best, inaccurate.

When a person with either an inaccurate mental picture of reality (due to past misperception) or little inner willingness to face present reality (due to its possible threat) tries to make sense of a brief tachistoscopic exposure, he is at the same disadvantage. If he sees what is on the screen, it doesn't fit too well with the picture of the world he knows. If he fears what he may see, he will narrow his field of vision to only a fraction of its normal scope. Either way he will not recognize what is flashed before his eyes as quickly as will the person for whom the real world is familiar and unthreatening. By simulating essentially what happens as our eyes jump this way and that in search of identifying clues to what we confront, the tachistoscope appears especially well suited to the task of identifying perceptual accuracy and inaccuracy in its most comprehensive sense.

The second line of evidence supporting this view is primarily logical, not psychological. Recognizing the fact that more anxiety-provoking stimuli than emotionally neutral stimuli are misperceived, there would seem to be no alternative explanation to the one already suggested. If words and pictures invested with various forms of emotional threat can rightfully represent social sources of threat, as seems evident from common observation and experimental findings, then it can be assumed that a subject tachistoscopically misperceives threatening stimuli because he generally misperceives threatening stimuli.

Social Perception Tests

The second major area of research in perceptual processes currently being carried on is concerned with social perception. By far the most common measure of social perception is a simple pencil-and-paper test that requires a subject to guess how a friend feels about him. As described by Goslin,[62] groups of approximately eleven friends rated one another on a standard questionnaire of personality traits. Each subject then predicted how the other group members had rated him. Social perception was scored as the simple difference between this prediction and the actual rating for each personality trait. In a variation of this design the author[63] scored the difference between peers' self-ratings and the predictions of these ratings. Dymond[64] combined both these types of peer prediction tasks. Rating groups numbered sixteen members, but only four members rated one another at a time, so that each person became a member of four subgroups in order to rate and be rated by every member.

A variety of pencil-and-paper instruments have been used for score prediction. In a subsequent study Dymond[65] had fifteen married couples predict one another's scores on one hundred and fifteen MMPI items. Belenky[66] administered the equally well-known Allport-Vernon Study of Values to small groups of fraternity brothers, scored the tests, and ranked each member for each of the six value areas. The subjects were then required to predict the ranking of each peer in each value area. Luft[67] had his subjects study transcripts of clinical interviews with two patients and predict the patients' answers to a sentence completion test of the multiple choice type. The difference between the predicted answers and the patients' actual answers was scored.

Using Drama

Cline and Richards[68] are to be credited with one of the most thorough and imaginative studies of this type. Twenty-five sound-color films were made of adults being interviewed at various public places. The adult "targets" received no prior warning. The interviewer questioned them about their personal values, feelings about themselves, hobbies, and the like. After the filmed interview, each target took a battery of personality tests including the MMPI, Strong Vocational Interest Blank, a word association test, and three administrations of a multiple-choice sentence completion test. In addition five close friends were interviewed and rated the target on a number of these same personality tests. Ten films that represented the broadest sampling of economic, social, racial, age, and other factors were finally selected. Then subjects viewed these films and filled out the tests the way they believed the targets had. The difference between the target's test answers and the subject's estimation of them was scored.

Less ambitious but interesting variations using live drama have been tried. Wrench and Endicott [69] had three actors stage a scene charged with many kinds of emotion. After watching it twice, the subjects rated various aspects of the drama for the type and degree of feelings shown. The ratings were scored for accuracy of perceived feeling. Bronfenbrenner[70] had his subjects participate in a series of two-person sociodramas. After each drama the subjects wrote down their impressions of the experience and then guessed what their partner had written. When transcriptions had been made of the written impressions of all subjects in the group, excerpts were extracted, and subjects were asked to identify those written by their partners. Again all scores were based on the difference between predicted and actual impressions.

Simple and Logical But—

The sheer simplicity of these measures of social perception makes them appealing. Most are easy to design, administer, and score. More important, perhaps, is the simplicity of the idea on which they are based. Few would question that the subject who comes close to correctly evaluating someone's thoughts, feelings, attitudes, and values perceives him more accurately than a subject who does not. Provided that the paper-and-pencil tests or dramas used to express these personal traits reflect accurately enough the important areas of human concern, there seems no apparent reason why the utmost confidence cannot be placed in the results of these tests.

Unfortunately, there are reasons for withholding full confidence. They by no means invalidate the method, but they do advise caution. There are a host of technical problems, most of which have to do with adjusting one person's use of a test rating scale to another's. Some rather complicated statistical operations are required to minimize these difficulties. At a more important level, the question has been raised as to whether there may not be other reasons for successfully predicting an acquaintance's test scores. For instance, group stereotypes may make it easy for group members to predict each other's scores. Or it may be as simple to attribute one's own feelings and thoughts to a target very much like oneself. In either event a prediction is made on the basis of something other than actual perceived differences between individuals yet is scored in the predictor's favor.

In an effort to provide some measure of control over these

and other possibilities for error, refinements of technique and scoring are constantly being attempted. The net result has been a greater sophistication of discrepancy score interpretation. It is perhaps too early to say whether this sophistication has made the social prediction method significantly more reliable, but the effort expended seems to indicate a faith that the problems are not insurmountable.

Safe and Unsafe Inferences

The discussion of empirical indicators in this chapter has been limited to two general types of measures. The question arises whether there might be other types by which the perceptual abilities of the mature Christian could be accurately identified. With perhaps the exception of the trained clinical worker's estimate of a subject's reality contact, there are not many other indicators to choose from. A smattering of self-report inventories and projectives claiming to measure perceptual characteristics can be found. Almost without exception, however, they leave something to be desired because of one common quality: they require that we *infer* perceptual accuracy or inaccuracy from something else— something like social prejudice or a tendency to project. All empirical indicators that claim to measure anything of importance require some inferences, but there must be some clear way to support them.

The most easily supportable inferences are those which generalize from a small but genuine instance of the exact quality being investigated to a broader manifestation of the same thing. For instance, when a subject misperceives a tachistoscopic exposure or fails to predict how an acquaintance has rated him on a questionnaire, this is *itself* an example of misperception. The only question to be asked is whether this is an isolated example of misperception. If it is, we have no right to claim that these two types of indicators measure "accurate perception" as fully as it is described in the first part of the chapter.

Considerable attention to this problem has been given in the discussion of both types of indicators. From the evidences available it would seem that substantial generalizations from the results of both instruments are warranted, expecially when their findings are the same.

IV

A Look Ahead

The next chapter will complete our "in depth" view of the mature Christian life. Perceiving reality implies some kind of response to it. Ethics is the traditional area of Christian theology that has attempted a description of this response. Yet the most important Christian ethics of our time comes from men who look to broader theological foundations. Christology is one of these foundations; Christian freedom is another. These and others will be drawn upon in the following pages in an effort to give empirical shape to the fluctuating pattern of mature Christian response.

NOTES

1. Luther, *Galatians 1-4*, pp. 191-92, 195.
2. Calvin, *Institutes*, ii.2, 13; ii.2, 15; i.4, 1.
3. Schleiermacher, *On Religion*, p. 36.
4. Barth, IV/1, 748.
5. Bonhoeffer, *Ethics*, pp. 197-98.
6. Barth, III/4, 585; Tillich, *Courage to Be*, p. 70.
7. Schleiermacher, *On Religion*, p. 127.
8. Calvin, *Institutes*, ii.2, 20.
9. Bonhoeffer, *Letters and Papers*, pp. 165-66.
10. Barth, IV/1, 102-3; cf. IV/1, 351-52; III/4, 4, 24, 586; IV/2, 50.
11. Reinhold Niebuhr, *Destiny*, pp. 69, 70; *Interpretation*, p. 149.
12. Reinhold Niebuhr, *Destiny*, p. 320.
13. Tillich, *Shaking of the Foundations*, p. 124; *Protestant Era*, pp. 74-75.
14. Num. 13.
15. Neil Sheehan, "Two Sides of Our Side," *New York Times Book Review*, May 14, 1967, p. 3.
16. Reinhold Niebuhr, *Destiny*, pp. 299, 319.
17. Bonhoeffer, *Ethics*, pp. 163-64.
18. Barth, IV/2, 745; cf. Bultmann, *Esistence and Faith*, p. 215; Tillich, *Systematic Theology*, III, 235.
19. Luther, *Galatians 5-6*, p. 103; Bultmann, *Existence and Faith*, pp. 30-31.
20. I Kings 22:1-23.
21. Reinhold Niebuhr, *Destiny*, pp. 65-66; H. Richard Niebuhr, *Revelation*, p. 101.
22. Bonhoeffer, *Cost of Discipleship*, p. 209.
23. Schleiermacher, *On Religion*, pp. 152-53, 180; *Christian Faith*, p. 561; Bultmann, *Essays*, pp. 13-14; Calvin, *Institutes*, iii.3, 7.
24. Bonhoeffer, *Life Together*, p. 63; cf. Tillich, *Systematic Theology*, III, 231-32.
25. Rom. 12:15.
26. Luke 10:38-42.
27. Matt. 19:16-30.
28. Luke 7:36-50.
29. Calvin, *Institutes*, iii.24, 12; cf. i.4, 1; ii.6, 1; also Reinhold Niebuhr, *Interpretation*, pp. 23-24; Bultmann, *Primitive Christianity*, pp. 186, 189.
30. Tillich, *Shaking of the Foundations*, p. 162, cf. pp. 57-58.
31. Calvin, *Institutes*, ii.2, 13.
32. Tillich, *Courage to Be*, p. 75.
33. *Ibid.*, p. 69.
34. Luther, *Galatians 1-4*, pp. 191-92.
35. Calvin, *Institutes*, i.17, 9.
36. Kierkegaard, *Training in Christianity*, pp. 62-64.
37. Tillich, *Protestant Era*, p. 79.

38. Kierkegaard, *Postscript*, p. 303.
39. Barth, IV/3(1), 468-69.
40. Bonhoeffer, *Letters and Papers*, pp. 165-66.
41. Barth, IV/2, 228; IV/3(1), 436.
42. Kierkegaard, *Works of Love*, p. 232.
43. Schleiermacher, *Christian Faith*, p. 138; Kierkegaard, *Postscript*, p. 498; Søren Kierkegaard, *Philosophical Fragments or a Fragment of Philosophy*, trans. David F. Swenson (Princeton: Princeton University Press, 1936), pp. 67-68; Bultmann, *Kerygma and Myth*, pp. 197-98.
44. Bultmann, *Existence and Faith*, p. 167.
45. Bonhoeffer, *Ethics*, p. 203.
46. Barth, IV/3(1), 452.
47. Reinhold Niebuhr, *Interpretation*, pp. 23-24.
48. H. Richard Niebuhr, *Revelation*, p. 101; cf. Reinhold Niebuhr, *Destiny*, pp. 65-66; *Nature*, p. 17.
49. Kierkegaard, *Works of Love*, p. 194; cf. Luther, *Galatians 1-4*, pp. 109, 434.
50. Reinhold Niebuhr, *Interpretation*, pp. 158-59.
51. Matt. 13:10-17; Mark 6:52.
52. Matt. 13:53-57.
53. Matt. 9:11; 12:1-2; *passim*.
54. Bultmann, *Existence and Faith*, p. 264.
55. Luther, *Galatians 5-6*, p. 103.
56. H. Richard Niebuhr, *Revelation*, p. 96.
57. Kierkegaard, *Postscript*, p. 209.
58. Barth, III/2, 375; IV/3(1), 452.
59. Tillich, *Shaking of the Foundations*, pp. 8-9.
60. Bultmann, *Existence and Faith*, p. 90, cf. p. 78; Luther, *Galatians 1-4*, p. 172.
61. Anne Mathews and Michael Wertheimer, "A 'Pure' Measure of Perceptual Defense Uncontaminated by Response Suppression," *Journal of Abnormal and Social Psychology*, LVII (1958), 373-76; Gerald S. Blum, "Perceptual Defense Revisited," *Journal of Abnormal and Social Psychology*, LI (1955), 24-29; Sherman E. Nelson, "Psychosexual Conflicts and Defenses in Visual Perception," *Journal of Abnormal and Social Psychology*, LI (1955), 427-33.
62. David A. Goslin, "Accuracy of Self-perception and Social Acceptance," *Sociometry*, XXV (1962), 283-96.
63. Duncombe, "The Evaluation of University Covenant Communities."
64. Rosalind F. Dymond, "Personality and Empathy," *Journal of Consulting Psychology*, XIV (1950), 343-50.
65. Rosalind F. Dymond, "Interpersonal Perception and Marital Hapness," *Canadian Journal of Psychology*, VIII (1954), 164-71.
66. Robert L. Belenky, "The Relationship Between Accuracy in Self-perception and the Perception of Others: A Study of Estimates of Performance on a Test of Values and a Test of Aspiration Level," *Dissertation Abstracts*, XX (1960), 3825-26.
67. Joseph Luft, "Implicit Hypotheses and Clinical Predictions," *Journal of Abnormal and Social Psychology*, XLV (1950), 156-60.

68. Victor B. Cline and James M. Richards, Jr., "Accuracy of Interpersonal Perception—a General Trait?" *Journal of Abnormal and Social Psychology*, LX (1960), 1-8.

69. David Wrench and Kirk Endicott, "Denial of Affect and Conformity," *Journal of Personality and Social Psychology*, I (1965), 484-86.

70. Urie Bronfenbrenner, *et al.*, "The Analysis of Social Sensitivity (Sympathy)," *American Psychologist*, VII (1952), 324.

---chapter VI---

DOING WHAT THE
SITUATION DEMANDS

I

Adequate Response and the Problem of Sin

The great religions of the world are addressed primarily
to problems of life. That is, they point to man's age-old
predicament—his bondage to life's "wrongness"—and pro-
claim a solution. The solution of Judaism and Christianity
is the Word of God. Out of the anguish of man's struggle
to free himself from the strangling consequences of his own
actions came the conviction that nothing less than divine
intervention could prevail against the power of sin. God's
saving Word for the Jew is embedded in the law and spoken
by the prophets. It chastises, encourages, blesses, and guides
a "stiff-necked" [1] people in the way they should go. So
directed by divine wisdom and faithfulness, the Jew learns
to do certain things and avoid doing others in order to
escape the enslaving power of sin. He responds to God's
Word by obedience to its commands.

Christianity claims to go one step further. Not only does the Christian respond to the written and spoken Word of God, but to the human life that perfectly embodies it. Jesus Christ is believed to be more than an inspired law-giver and prophet through whom God speaks to man—more even than a perfect example of humanity and conduct to be imitated. The so-called "unique" Christian claim is that bondage to sin is broken only as one responds faithfully to the man Jesus Christ. It is the response of one person to another that redeems. The Christian realizes his full humanity by means of God's humanity in Jesus Christ, the incarnate Word of God. Victory over sin comes not so much from following never changing eternal truths as from possessing the freedom to respond appropriately to the always changing world in which the spirit of Christ is at work.

As with most sweeping theological differences, the historial reality it reflects is less clear-cut. In attempting to escape what it felt to be the stultifying legalism of Judaism, early Christianity stumbled often into ways and beliefs hardly less restrictive of genuine human freedom. Some Christians attempted a slavish imitation of Jesus. Others set for themselves impossible ideals of Christian virtue and piety. The words of Jesus and the evangelists have been used to justify both asceticism and debauchery, selfless altruism and cynical power, scrupulous pacifism and mass murder. In the name of Christianity nearly every excess of mind or body known to man has been committed. Such excesses are by no means typical of all movements or periods in Christian history. Yet it was difficult for so powerful a church not to provide fertile ground for insensitive human relations, legalistic teachings, and rote interpretations. It was against this dehumanization as much as anything that the Protestant reform took shape.

The Vision of the Reformers

Typical of most movements of protest and reform, Protestantism from the beginning was plagued with serious discrepancies between ideals and practice. While espousing Christian freedom, Protestant churches often became as legalistic as the worst of medieval Christianity. And yet as one reads the reformers and tries to grasp the spirit that moved them, it is their ability to see beyond their own limitations that is so impressive. Like the aged and infirm Moses on Mt. Nebo, gazing upon the promised land, the reformers could point to what they themselves would never attain. Perhaps it is only in the wilderness that great theologians live and die. Perhaps it is their own sickness, the ebbing of their spiritual life, that allows them to see so clearly the basis for sound health and new life. For it was in the vision, and not in the faltering steps, of the reformers that the basic Christian understanding of adequate human response was rekindled for a modern age.

Adequate response in Protestant thought is largely defined by the relationship of faith and works. The reformers removed good works from the economy of salvation and made them instead a possibility of the life of faith. While no less necessary, good works became the mark (and not the precondition) of the mature Christian life. Both Luther and Calvin insisted that the Christian's response to the world is from the heart and corresponds with the realities and responsibilities that faith reveals. Of the two, Calvin had more definite ideas about which works are appropriate expressions of faith and which are not. Luther tended to stress the Christian's freedom from false belief and opinion. Yet the two reformers shared the conviction that only genuine faith provides that inner strength by which a man is free— free from the bonds of sin, free from rigid inner scruples and inflexible social expectations, free even from the strictures of the law.

Contemporary Protestant theology has given this basic insight a more positive expression. Instead of describing faith mainly as something that frees one *from* bondage to a crippling power, the emphasis today is upon a faith that frees one *for* involvement in the world. As a result there has been a gradual shift in the function of individual redemption. Where it once was seen primarily as the end or goal of the Christian life, today Christians are more apt to see it as a means of responding sensitively to the will of God and the needs of the world. In the biblical idiom it is a talent to be invested and not hoarded. Behind this growing attitude is no disparagement of the need for individual redemption, but rather a renewed awareness that the gift of inward liberation both enables and demands an active participation in the redemption of others. Christ works through the man of faith to redeem not only him, but his neighbor and his society also. In this respect the Christian's responsibility toward others can be discharged only to the extent of his ability to respond adequately to the needs of others.

Traditionally no single doctrine has been able to express this concern for adequate response. Owing largely to polemic interests, a virtual doctrine was created by the reformers to condemn compulsive, inflexible, and otherwise inappropriate behavior. But as the urgency to counter the "wicked" and corrupt [2] doctrines of the medieval church subsided, so too did the need for giving these behaviors doctrinal importance. Today Protestantism regards as its greatest enemy not a rival church, but its own failure to understand and respond to a rapidly changing world. As suggested in the previous chapter, inadequate understanding points to a failure of perception central to the doctrine of revelation. Failure of appropriate response may or may not be a direct result of misperception, but doctrinally it is most often seen as a problem in ethics. Significantly there seems to be the same dialectical relationship between perception and response as between revelation and ethics. While this equates neither response and ethics nor perception and revelation, Protestant theology has yet to affirm an ethic of Christian responsibility that does not presuppose the ability to respond fully and appropriately to the world.

A Multi-doctrinal Approach

Current thought in this area of Christian ethics is informed by many traditional doctrines. Among the most important of these seem to be the doctrines of justification by faith, Christian freedom, and sanctification. Each in its own way projects the image of the man whose inward liberation from sin frees him to be outwardly responsive. Justification by faith serves to explain why the Christian feels secure enough within himself to let go of all false securities. Christian freedom describes the way in which his actions, behavior, or "works" follow naturally and appropriately from this freeing sense of security. And sanctification is concerned with the Christian's steady growth in both these areas as well as with the moral value of this growth. All three doctrines bear upon the nature of human response.

Obviously, then, there are many doctrinal paths to adequate response in Protestant thought. The paths often cross and parallel one another, and one must choose the doctrine that seems best to catch the essence of adequate response in Christian terms. The writer's preference is for the doctrine of Christian freedom, possibly because it seems to encourage simple and unadorned descriptions of how the man of faith acts. It is almost as if under the aegis of Christian freedom theologians themselves feel freer to pursue their natural interests in concrete human behavior.

It would also seem that Christian freedom is the one constant theme running throughout the whole of Protestant thought concerning the human effects of justification by faith. Whether justification by faith is interpreted primarily in terms of a person's new knowledge, belief, or feeling, it radically affects his former pattern of dependence. What he does is no longer controlled by personal scruples, others' expectations, driving passions, or unreasonable fears. He becomes free to respond faithfully to Christ, and through him, to those to whom Christ ministers. This is the ethics of justification; but because of the radically freeing effect of justification, it must also be seen as the ethics of the sanctified life. Through the renewal of his actions the mature Christian becomes the witness and the work of redeemed humanity. By the fact of his redeemed humanity he enters actively into the redemptive work of Christ.

Just how the mature Christian responds to the world is not described in a few pages. But those which follow should suggest a number of features in his everyday behavior that set him apart from others.

II

The "Fitting Response" [3]

There is a kind of person who is able to respond to the world in a way that does justice to the infinite variety of its living and natural forms. He does what each situation calls for, regardless of what he or others did before. He is free to strike out on unchartered paths when the occasion warrants. He can try new ways of doing things in familiar situations and responds in a way appropriate to each situation. While adaptable and flexible in all his dealings with the world, he is as equally at home in a routinized existence as he is living with few established bench marks.

The mature Christian is an active participant in the world. This means that he takes his cue from what is going on about him. Of course this presupposes a correct knowledge of the situation, a knowledge which begins with accurate perception. But appropriate response is more than accurate perception. The mature Christian supplies a "fitting response to what is happening." [4] The action fits with the end he desires and the situation he encounters. Neither his desires nor the exigencies of the situation alone dictate how he responds.

The Subtle "How"

The world to which the mature Christian responds is the same everyday world we all know so well. There are no special times or special places where Christian maturity makes no difference. The mature Christian is to be found in every walk of life. He can be employed or unemployed, student or teacher, hippie or square, doctor or patient, child or parent, soldier or conscientious objector, churchman or Sunday-morning golfer. The mature Christian is distinguished less by what he does than by how he does it.[5] His freeing sense of security allows him to do everything more responsively. Nor is this sense of security revealed by "a glance, a look, a gesture," but in the common "living movement and representative action" of daily life.[6] "His appearance is precisely like that of other men" to the ordinary observer; there is no "outward difference by which recognition could be effected" except by someone able to "experimentally observe" the way he acts.[7]

The key to understanding and observing mature Christian response, therefore, lies in the appropriateness of response. Whether there is or is not anything eye-catching about what he does, the mature Christian possesses the unique ability "to do what is necessary at the given place and with a due consideration of reality." [8] Here as elsewhere, knowing the reality of a situation is basic to any ensuing action. "A correct appreciation of the real situation," especially the "more complex actual situations of a man's life," implies its own necessities for action once a particular goal is recognized.[9] What is necessary to accomplish a goal can involve an infinite variety of actions, but it is something that at a particular moment works best to remove the actual difficulties preventing success. Simply put, appropriate response is a step in the right direction toward whatever end or goal desired. It is the most "sensible and useful" of all possible responses, and to the mature Christian it is what "the object demands, that which is proper to him in the fact of this object." [10]

The Christian Postman

An extended example may help to clarify what is meant. For the moment disregard the particularly social or interpersonal aspects of appropriate response and concentrate upon those having mainly to do with accomplishing a task. Consider what might be distinctive about the way a mature Christian mail carrier would handle himself and his job on a trying day.

Our postman leaves his apartment for work at the usual hour. Somewhat absentmindedly he presses the elevator button and waits. Nothing happens. The light indicates that it is still at the ground floor, and another press of the button fails to move it. What he might do at this juncture depends on the situation. For instance, he may decide to walk down (if there are stairs and if it is quick enough), use another elevator (if there is one), or call the superintendent (if that has gotten results before). What he *won't* do is to continue pressing the button, quietly wait, kick the door, or swear a blue streak—unless any of these responses have a reasonable expectation of fetching the elevator.

He arrives at the bus stop without his usual few minutes to spare. No bus is in sight. How long he waits depends on what information he can glean quickly (Did the bus leave? Is it late? Is his watch slow?) and the alternatives open to him. Whatever he does will be appropriate to the situation, although in retrospect he may realize that another response would have better relieved the difficulty. The situation may frustrate or anger him, but it doesn't affect in any essential way the course of action he chooses. He won't become rattled and panicked. He won't wait indefinitely or leave immediately. Nor does he hop the next bus to stop (which turns out to be headed for another part of town).

Arriving at work ten minutes late, our postman learns that the man with whom he shares his route has called in sick. After a few appropriate curses (optional), he settles down to his initial task of sorting mail for the route. With twice as much to accomplish by 10:00 A.M., he must decide how best he can do the work. Can he get some help? Should he sort for only his own deliveries? Would it be wise to deliver only first class mail today? Gauging the importance of each alternative and the amount of time it should take, he decides on one and sets his pace. Twenty minutes later he discovers that he has miscased two pieces of mail and is faced with the decision of checking futher or continuing on. A possibly different set of priorities comes into play, but again his response is one that makes the best of a bad situation. This postman may not have a great deal of native intelligence, stamina, or speed, but he uses what he has without getting tied up in knots or impulsively doing the first thing that comes to mind. He is simply "adapting himself to the realities of life." [11]

After closing out with a few minutes to spare, our postman grabs a quick cup of coffee, packs his bag, and begins his morning deliveries. Having had to decide which mail would be delivered to whom at the time of sorting, he looks forward to a less trying round. His hopes are marred by the late arrival of two special delivery letters, but he decides on a way to alter his route to include them.

The second special delivery is a fourth-floor walk up. No one answers. He is writing out the attempt-to-deliver notice when he smells gas. He knocks again with no result and then calls. The gas odor is still there, but no stronger than usual hallway odors.

Already behind schedule, he begins to push the notice under the door when he decides that this is not enough. He tries the door and then attempts to force it, both without success. At the risk of appearing foolish, or at best delaying his planned deliveries, he sets about to save a possible gas victim. Enlisting the aid of the tenants across the way, the superintendant and the police are called, a fire escape entry investigated, the building gas line shut off, and an electric drill for the lock located. As it turns out, the fire escape provides the quickest entry, and the rest is unnecessary. In a sense the whole venture is unnecessary since the apartment proves to be unoccupied. But given the particular situation, the whiff of gas, a locked door, the type of neighborhood, and his own inner hunch—the postman's response is necessary and appropriate. It is the only response that accords with reality as he perceives it, and thus the "only . . . thing he can do." [12]

Responsive, Not Responsible, Action

How the mature Christian responds to a series of situations such as this cannot be easily summed up by words like "level-headed," "heroic," or even "compassionate." He may be all of these, but were he not somehow "inwardly liberated," "free for the tasks of the day," [13] the performance would appear forced and unnatural. Perhaps the word "responsible" comes closer to describing this quality of Christian response. Insofar as it implies the ability to "respond to all actions upon" him, a kind of "elasticity of behavior" in a rapidly changing situation, it is apt.[14] But "responsible" can sound moralistic. The unique element in the postman's behavior was not that he acted to save a human life, but that his act to save a human life (or to efficiently deliver the mail) "flow[ed] forth" or "follow[ed]" naturally from his appraisal of the situation.[15] "Good works do not make a good man, but a good man does good works." [16]

The difference between moralistic "responsible" behavior and what we might describe as natural "responsive" behavior is especially important in the realm of personal relations. The mature Christian responds to the "actions of other beings," [17] not to a preconceived notion about them. While his actions may be informed by a set of values or beliefs, his "responsiveness" is more a freedom of action in applying these values and beliefs than a restricting of action because of them. True responsiveness describes the way in which "the self relates itself in its freedom to other selves." [18] It involves human "identification," "real communication," self-giving, and a kind of "freedom in fellowship." The Christian transcends both "egotism and altrusim" with respect to his neighbor and "honors him as a man." [19] Like the Good Samaritan, he allows himself to be guided by what he sees rather than by a prior expectation of conduct insensitive to human realities.[20]

In the Home

The family situation may provide the best context for observing human response. Responses to others outside the home or to difficulties on the job are probably modeled after responses made in more intense and personal family relationships. As a father, the mature Christian wears the mantle of social expectations, yet "in a way that is completely free" and "at full liberty either to use or omit them." [21] When he senses, for example, that a disciplinary role would not result in the "right act" toward his son, he does something else. He "does not care what the world says about him" nor "depend on the judgment of others." [22] He can occasionally step outside a certain paternal role without fear of violating its integrity, as did the father who "ran and embraced" his prodigal son.[23]

More often today it is the son who has difficulty being truly responsive toward his father. Christian maturity in the young may outwardly appear rough around the edges, but it springs from the same freeing sense of security "from which all decent action flows." [24] As he grows older, the relationship with his father undergoes change. Where he would most appropriately laugh at his father's corny jokes at age nine, at nineteen he may be truer to himself—and to his father—if he shoots back a sarcastic remark. Years later, with a family of his own, he will have a still different relationship to his father. Without forgetting his continuing dependence upon him, the mature Christian will nevertheless respond sensitively to his father's own need for filial understanding and support. It may well be that once again he finds it "fitting" [25] to laugh at the same jokes—or perhaps to concoct a few of his own in return. With each passing year and each new event the situation changes. How one will respond to the other is "not at all understandable apart from that situation." [26]

Of all the family relationships the most fundamental is undoubtedly between husband and wife. Sexuality is an important element in this, but its importance cannot be understood apart from the condition of partnership. In marriage mature Christians respond to one another out of their mutual love and respect. There is a common sharing, an assumed equality, in which each is "for the other." [27] Such interpersonal response reflects the depth and subtlety of feeling. A nod of the head may be as appropriate as a lengthy dissertation. There is no lack of formal expectations and obligations that inform their behavior toward one another, but mature Christian marriage partners "obey from the heart" [28] to fulfill both the letter and the spirit of the law. They respond to the need they sense in the other for a particular kind of support or companionship at a particular time. "To long for the transcendent when you are in your wife's arms, is, to put it mildly, lack of taste." [29]

In family relations as well as in all other aspects of his daily life the mature Christian puts first things first. What he does is appropriate to the "concrete present." [30]

A Slave to "His Oaths and His Guests" [31]

There is also a kind of person whose actions are more in the nature of reactions than responses. Like a dull and unimaginative pupil, his answers to life are "established in advance" [32] by rote and formula. In each new situation his response is primarily to its old and familiar aspects and not to that which makes it unique. There is a noticeable "hardening and inflexibility" of his actions in unfamiliar or threatening circumstances.[33] Yet the most obvious limitation is his ineffectiveness as a person. He botches all but the most routinized jobs and is capable of only superficial human relationships. He does the right thing at the wrong time and accomplishes nothing of consequence. His life is one of "false doing," and his essential responses to life are "inappropriate." [34]

An Inner "Drivenness"

Equally distinctive is the way in which this kind of person performs his limited repertoire. He acts as if he were being "driven," as if he dared not risk a new response. There is a certain mustness about everything he does. He seems "compelled" to go through the motions without being able to break free, to "cling to the shadows" as in a "prison of self-possession."[35] Whatever is done is performed "rigidly and perfunctorily," "dependently or slavishly," never freely.[36] Something seems to have a "secret hold on him." He is "a slave to his work" and in "bondage to an alien self."[37] In times of stress, uncertainty, and threat, his driven manner is especially noticeable.

It appears that this person is responding more to inner needs than to outer realities—as though he were so intent upon obeying a voice from within that situational differences were of little consequence. He may be a man of excessive scruples who feels that he must do certain things regardless of actual consequences and who thus finds himself "drawn as if by extraneous impulse" to do "absurd and ridiculous works."[38] If so, he is likely to appear "prudent, cautious, diffident, and law-abiding," given to a "mistrustful surveillance and appraisal of everything" or to a "timidly over-scrupulous subordination" of normal situations.[39] Although he may not be aware of it, he will studiously avoid the excitable, the chaotic, and the undisciplined. If the restricted forms and compulsive quality seem odd to other people, he may not be insensitive to this; but he finds himself incapable of altering them without an "uneasy conscience," considerable fear, and anxiety or racking doubt.[40]

Entangled in the Net

For example, such a person is inordinately bothered when the "minutiae of social and moral standards" are threatened.[41] If he is a regular church or lodge member, he may be conscience-stricken by even the thought of missing a week's attendance. What begins as a "scruple of conscience" leads inevitably to the point where he is "tortured in . . . conscience and brought into bondage." [42]

For when once the conscience is entangled in the net, it enters a long and inextricable labyrinth, from which it is afterward most difficult to escape. When a man begins to doubt whether it is lawful for him to use linen for sheets, shirts, napkins and handkerchiefs, he will not long be secure as to hemp, and will at last have doubts as to tow. . . . In fine, he will come to this, that he will deem it criminal to trample on a straw lying in his way. . . . When men are involved in such doubts, whatever be the direction in which they turn, everything they see must offend their conscience.[43]

In an effort to appease his conscience other inappropriate behavior is "made necessary." [44] Such a man feels that he "must achieve something" and sets out on an "idolatrous pursuit of false securities and redemptions," yet "he can never find enough works to make his conscience peaceful." [45] Something like this is pictured in Jesus' denunciatory descriptions of Pharisees who "have neglected the weightier matters of the law . . . straining out a gnat and swallowing a camel!" [46] Nor does it matter if his inappropriate behavior remains hidden or is seen by others. This "strange 'law in his limbs,' an irresistible compulsion," effectively blocks the kind of response to the world that is "necessary, profitable, and salutary" for everyday living.[47]

In the civic and moral sphere he is equally inflexible. He is the kind of person who could not dishonor his nation's flag to save his country. Nor could he bring himself to commit adultery if his marriage depended upon it.[48] As if harboring hidden doubts about his own loyalties and moral purity, he feels insecure until certain hard and fast rules are prescribed and followed. He dares not allow an exception to these, whether in public or private, for himself or for others. Lacking the deep inner security of the mature Christian, he tries "vainly to meet the social perplexities of a complex civilization with irrelevant precepts." [49] The more involved the issue, the more inappropriate the response.

Other-Directedness

The inner voice to which he attends may also be tuned to what other people think and say about him. Whereas the mature Christian lives in "freedom from human judgments and evaluations," he seeks "social approval" and the "esteem of his fellows." [50] As such, he experiences "the peculiar fear or dread that always openly or secretly dominates the man who has a hunger for recognition." [51] Rather than being rigidly inner-directed, his responses are now slavishly "other-directed." [52] They may vary with the given situation but only with that part of the total situation that touches his self-esteem.

To the degree that the opinion of others becomes his main concern, his public life may differ markedly from his private life. When in the company of those whose good opinion and acceptance he seeks, his behavior conforms to their norms and expectations. He displays remarkable flexibility in adapting himself to the varying standards of different groups or persons, but not to genuine situational variations. Nevertheless, in private he may be quite capable of making appropriate discriminations and can generally be expected to do what each situation demands. For this reason Jesus described some of the Pharisees also as "hypocrites" who "do all their deeds to be seen by men." They are like those who "cleanse the outside of the cup" but are quite able to tolerate a soiled interior as long as others are unaware of it.[53]

Herod and John

Regardless of whether such a person attends more closely to an inflexible conscience or to the views of others, his actions are less informed by the concrete present than by a rule of conduct established in advance. In either case there is a mechanical necessity about his behavior, a drivenness or compulsion which allows neither for genuine free choice nor for creative response.[54] Often both orientations come together to reinforce a particularly inappropriate act, as was the case in the beheading of John the Baptist. King Herod imprisoned John at the instigation of his wife but respected him as a "righteous and holy man" and "heard him gladly." Nevertheless, he had John beheaded "because of his oaths and his guests." [55]

Like Herod, the man who is unable to respond adequately to the total context of a situation finds himself the victim of "his oaths and his guests." Even as a king he is driven to humble himself before the whims of his subjects, of his conscience, or both. He is without the freedom to decide or act for himself. What he does is directed by "forces in the body and the mind, but not the self as self." [56] Faced with threat or unfamiliar circumstances, he is rigid and inflexible, resisting change and slow to learn. Thus he finds it difficult to form meaningful friendships, to establish a normal family life, to love someone, and to genuinely give himself to persons in need.[57] He lives a lonely life, a stranger and an outcast in his own kingdom.

Responsive Versus Reactive

As with all other characteristics of the mature Christian life discussed in this book, the distinction between those who manifest such a life and those who do not is ultimately a distinction between a freeing sense of security and its absence. Because the mature Christian feels secure within himself, he lives in "increasing freedom." [58] His day-to-day behavior is "free from legal prescription and human convention." [59] Each response to the world is a "fitting action," something that "arises with the given situation" and is "in the true sense 'in accordance with reality.' " [60] It is the kind of security that allows a man to "plunge himself into the life of a godless world without attempting to gloss over . . . or . . . transfigure it." [61]

Without this inner freedom a man must always be looking to himself—his own "works," whatever they may be.[62] He is "possessed" by the need to act in a certain way toward the world and thus is caught in "endless repetitions" of the same behavior.[63] Only secondarily comes his response to the immediate world that confronts him; it is first and foremost to the promptings of an inner voice that demands rigid obedience in return for the promise of a longed-for security. Whether "acting under the pressures of the need for recognition" or a "scruple of conscience," he is "not free to act as the situation demands." [64] When a man must "look right and left" [65] before he can look straight ahead, he no longer is a responsive human being.

III

Some Indicators of Adequate Response

Living as we do at a time of heightened interest in mental health and emotional adjustment, we are used to hearing about techniques of personality assessment. Most of these techniques are designed to assess how a person responds to his environment. Literally thousands of tests and measures have been devised to tell us how adequately a person can perform in different kinds of situations. All these indicators presume some standard of appropriate behavior against which a person's actual responses are compared. The job is to separate from this mass of reported tests and measures those which seem best to tap the characteristics of the mature Christian described above.

"True" or "False"?

One of the simplest approaches devised is the peer-rating instrument. Inappropriate response does not often escape the eye of the careful observer, even if he is without special training. This may be due largely to the fact that among the five types of behavioral characteristics considered in this book, inappropriate response most directly affects other people. When the observer is himself one of those affected (as he is in a peer-rating situation), it is more than likely that the subject who responds to others without regard for actual, discernible differences will be seen in essentially the same way by all observers.

For example, the author[66] had groups of five to seven close friends rate each other on items such as: "He does what each situation itself calls for," "He is more capable than most of deep friendships," "He sometimes seems to act as if he were being driven and not free," and "He responds in a way appropriate to each new thing." Each of these descriptions, often in the same words, can be found in the preceding section of this chapter. Conceivably, every descriptive statement in that section could be put in a similar form and used in a peer-rating instrument. When a half-dozen friends or associates can essentially agree on how well such a statement fits a particular person, there is good reason to take it seriously.

Self-rating instruments have shown themselves to be effective in identifying response adequacy too. Most persons can and will describe how they respond with a fair amount of accuracy. There are reasons for this. One is that patterns of response are more likely to be noticed by the subject himself than are patterns of perceptual or expressive behavior. In addition, many forms of inadequate response have assumed cultural respectability and are therefore not apt to be denied. And even where the subject has some awareness that his behavior is inappropriate, he may feel sufficiently well protected by culturally accepted rationalizations to freely report it.

Among the most widely used self-rating or self-report measures of response adequacy is the Wesley Rigidity Scale.[67] According to the designer, rigidity is a "tendency to persist in responses that may previously have been suitable in some situation or other, but no longer appear adequate to achieve current goals or solve current problems." [68] The scale consists of fifty items rated for rigid behavior by five out of five clinical judges. Some sample items are: "I am often the last one to give up trying to do a thing," "I would not like the kind of work which involves a large number of different activities," "I dislike having to learn new ways of doing things," and "There is usually only one best way to solve most problems."

Another way to have a person describe his behavior is to have him fill out an attitude scale. If the scale is properly designed, one can infer that his attitudes about certain things reflect his general behavior toward them. A good example is the popular California F Scale.[69] Most F Scale items indicate attitudes reflecting inappropriate responses to emotionally laden situations: "Obedience and respect for authority are the most important virtues children should learn," "An insult to our honor should always be punished," "People can be divided into two distinct classes: the weak and the strong." These items express, in socially acceptable form, the general tendency of the authoritarian personality to rely more upon culturally sanctioned forms of behavior than upon varying situational factors.

Problems and Games

Apart from what other people will report about him, or what a subject will report about himself, there are a host of fascinating experimental situations that allow direct observation of a subject's responses to a variety of situations.

For many years one of the standard performance measures of rigid response has been the Einstellung problem. As described by Luchins,[70] the subject is given fourteen problems to solve, in each of which he is asked to measure out a specified number of quarts of liquid given three containers of various capacities. For example, the first problem requires the subject to show how he would measure out 31 quarts if he were given a 20-quart jar, a 59-quart jar, and a 4-quart jar. The next five problems are in the same form $(x = b - a - 2c)$. Problems 7 through 13 are of such a nature that they can be solved either by this "long" form or by a "short" form $(x = a - c)$. The last problem can be solved only by the short form. The subject is given two and one-half minutes to solve each problem and is informed that he need not use all the containers.

There are a number of ways of scoring the Einstellung problem. Luchins scores for elapsed time and appropriateness of method as well as for whether the final problem is solved. In a twelve-problem version of the task, Ainsworth[71] uses a score based upon the problem at which the subject switches to the short form. That is, if a subject uses the long form for only those problems that require it, he is given the highest score. The next highest score is given for using the long form for only one problem that could have been solved by the shorter form. A lower score is given for each succeeding use of the long form, and the lowest for using the long form when it is also an incorrect method. However the problem is scored, the rigid person is said to be the one who perseveres in the originally rewarded solution despite its increasing inappropriateness.

A popular variation of this principle has been incorporated into a card game. As described by Welsey,[72] the Wisconsin Card Sorting Task (WCST) consists of a deck of cards on which are printed four standard symbols (triangle, circle, square, and cross) in four different colors and in four different denominations (number of symbols per card). Some versions of the game add different colored borders as well. The experimenter privately selects a concept ("symbol," "color," "denomination," etc.) and challenges the subject to guess what it is. The subject sorts the deck of cards into four bins marked by four cards (face up), guided only by the experimenter's indication on each placement that the card is "right" or "wrong." After ten consecutive placements judged "right," the experimenter switches his concept unannounced. The number of cards required to establish a criterion of ten correct placements according to this new concept is then scored. The same scoring is used for the final concept or concepts.

Another measure of general rigidity and perseveration is the Color-Word Test.[73] The subject is asked to read as quickly as possible ten lines of ten words each. Each word is the name of a color and is printed in black type. On the next page appear ten rows of ten asterisks printed in various colors. The subject is asked to "read" the colors as quickly as possible. On the last page are printed ten lines of ten color-naming words printed in inappropriate colors. Here the subject is instructed to "read" the color and ignore the word meaning. Scored are the reading time and number of errors on the last page as they differ from his reading time and number of errors on the first two pages.

Because it can be claimed that these problem-solving type

tests may favor subjects with a high I.Q. or considerable practice in doing exercises of this sort, it is often wise to administer a standard intelligence test as a check. Another check is to bypass I.Q. and practice entirely with a different type of test, such as the one described by Frenkel-Bruns-wik.[74] Here the subject is given a series of pictures in booklet form. On the first page the picture is clearly that of a dog, but with each successive page the pictured figure begins to assume increasingly the proportions of a cat. The subject is asked to identify the kind of animal appearing on each page. Responses of the typically flexible subject will begin to evidence doubt about the identity of the pictured animal within a few pages. But the rigid subject will cling tenaciously to his dog responses, sometimes until the very last picture.[75]

Again, the Moving Light

One previously discussed design employing the unusual autokinetic effect (pp. 50-51) showed a similar result. Reasoning that the rigid subject would hold onto an established pattern of autokinetic movement after the effect had been stabilized, Millon[76] scored the number of trials required before a subject established a pattern with respect to distance and direction of apparent light movement. Having achieved a criterion of ten out of thirteen trials in a particular pattern, he introduced a second light. The common effect of this light is to prevent the occurrence of the autokinetic effect or to quickly extinguish it once the effect has been experienced. All subjects took the California F Scale and half were given the type of instructions (ego-involving) which place the subject under stress.

The results were dramatic. Those under stress who scored high (socially rigid, authoritarian) on the F Scale not only established a pattern five times more quickly than low scorers under stress, but tended to persist in this pattern more than did the lows after the second light was introduced. The study illustrates the nature of the relationship between intolerance of ambiguity and rigidity. In being the first to establish a norm, the high F subjects were attempting to structure an ambiguous situation; and in being the last to relinquish the norm, they were not responding in an appropriate manner to the changed stimulus. They acted much like the subjects in the Frenkel-Brunswik experiment who continued to treat the stimulus as a dog long after it had become a cat.

Other-directed Conformity

A rich field of experimental work also touching the concerns of this chapter has to do with persuasibility and other-directed behavior. Inappropriate yielding to social pressure is a fairly simple thing to test and has encouraged the design of some imaginative testing situations. In the typical design a subject is asked to respond in an appropriate manner to various presented stimuli. Unknown to him, his testing group includes one or more planted stooges whom he may or may not know personally. The stooges respond to the presented stimuli inappropriately. Seeing others respond differently, the subject is subtly tempted to alter his pattern of response in accord. Sometimes he is aware that he is being influenced; most often he is not.

One of the best social-yielding situations was reported by Dittes and Kelly.[77] The experimenters offered a prize to the group of subjects "best in efficiency, smoothness of working together, and soundness of decision." Among the tasks required was a number judgment problem in which eleven successive pairs of dot-filled squares were presented. Group members judged privately which square of each pair contained more dots, but were told that the correct answer would be the same for every pair. Since the prize was contingent upon both group consensus and accuracy, subjects were allowed to communicate by note with other members. Notes were intercepted (by the experimenters) and fictitious ones substituted which gave each subject the impression that all other members of his group had found the first square of each pair to contain the most dots. As judgments became progressively simpler (realistically possible), it became apparent that the second square contained more dots. Subjects responded with both a private and a public decision between every pair, and were scored for their degree of conformity with the fictitious (and incorrect) group norm.

Such experimental designs go a long way toward simulating life situations. We see in this design, for instance, a high degree of group interaction, stress, and the arousal of affiliation and achievement motives within the context of an actual social situation. The subject forgets that he is in a laboratory and being observed and feels keenly the social pressure not to alter his public (and often private) response to an increasingly obvious error of factual judgment. Were this design further refined to discriminate more sensitively between appropriate and inappropriate yielding to other's views, as has been done elsewhere,[78] it would prove an extremely useful measure of adequate response.

One of the newer fields of experimental research, known as cognitive dissonance, deals with the relationship between behavior and belief. Festinger[79] and Brehm and Cohen[80] report that persons who are offered just enough incentive to act against a personal belief and yet who perceive this act to have been freely chosen are more likely than those not meeting these conditions to change their belief in the direction of their act. For such a person this new belief becomes both the present justification and further incentive for behavior which is neither freely decided nor responsive to reality. On the other hand, the subject who sees how he is influenced to act in a way discrepant with his belief is less likely to change this belief, rationalize his acts, or change his subsequent pattern of behavior because of it.

The Limits of Response Measures

While not always separable theoretically or practically, two general types of empirical measures have been described above: those which measure rigidity and inflexibility and those which measure inappropriate conformity to either inward or outward standards of conduct. Few characteristics described in the previous section of this chapter would not be tapped by one or more instruments described in this section. But the area of adequate response is an extremely broad one; it would be foolish to suppose that each appropriate and inappropriate response behavior mentioned can be empirically identified with the same reliability.

Despite the plethora of tests, measures, and designs that purport to test response adequacy, the person who has the time and patience to plow through the published literature on present research will discover at least two major weaknesses that call for remedy. First, there is a decided lack of good measures discriminating behavior influenced by sensitive moral principles from behavior which is moralistic, scrupulous, and driven. Some of the better rating scales and inventories do catch a piece of this. Certainly clinical observation can make the distinction. But comparatively little attention has been given this important area by mainline research. One often wonders why.

The other weakness, for which there may be no remedy at all, is a weakness that pervades much of modern-day testing. This is the undue emphasis placed upon the pathological and abnormal. It is much easier to conceptualize, talk about, and test for things like rigidity, perseveration, social yielding, drivenness, scrupulousness and compulsiveness than whatever it is that constitutes freedom from these crippling characteristics. Empirical identification of these characteristics may tell us who is not a mature Christian, but we do not establish the presence of health by showing the absence of disease. While the problem certainly touches every characteristic of the mature Christian personality discussed in this book, it is most noticeable where adequate response is concerned.

Future testers, among whom hopefully may be a few theologians, will have to grapple with these problems. There has been a start, a good start, toward nailing down in empirical fashion some of the most salient characteristics of adequate response. The measures described here will separate the sheep from the goats—if there are not too many shades of gray between.

IV

Putting It Together

We have arrived at the point where it is appropriate to ask some probing questions about what all this means. The concluding chapter will be disappointing to those who hope for convincing theological arguments supporting the five sets of polar descriptions presented or their suggested empirical measures. Likewise, those who look for a formula by which to integrate the numerous empirical measures into a do-it-yourself testing program for their churches will find little benfit in reading further. What is offered in these final pages is something of the writer's own thinking about the theological and empirical problems encountered. Red flags no doubt went up from time to time for most attentive readers; the last chapter will be an attempt to respond to some of them.

NOTES

1. Exod. 32:9.
2. Luther, *Galatians 1-4*, pp. 91-92.
3. H. Richard Niebuhr, *Responsible Self*, p. 67.
4. *Ibid.*
5. Kierkegaard, *Postscript*, p. 544.
6. Kierkegaard, *Fear and Trembling*, pp. 49-51; Schleiermacher, *Christian Faith*, pp. 10-11.
7. Kierkegaard, *Postscript*, pp. 446, 451, 442.
8. Bonhoeffer, *Ethics*, pp. 197-98.
9. *Ibid.*, p. 327.
10. Bultmann, *Essays*, p. 44; Barth, IV/1, 742.
11. Bonhoeffer, *Letters and Papers*, p. 129.
12. Barth, IV/1, 748; cf. IV/2, 783.
13. Bultmann, *Essays*, p. 60; *Existence and Faith*, pp. 181-82.
14. H. Richard Niebuhr, *Responsible Self*, p. 126; Bonhoeffer, *Letters and Papers*, p. 138.
15. Martin Luther, "The Freedom of a Christian," trans. W. A. Lambert, *Career of the Reformer I*, ed. Harold J. Grimm ("Luther's Works," Vol. XXXI; Philadelphia: Muhlenberg, 1957), p. 367; Luther, *Galatians 5-6*, p. 127; cf. *Galatians 1-4*, p. 255.
16. Luther, "Freedom of a Christian," p. 361, cf. p. 349; cf. also *Galatians 1-4*, p. 376; Martin Luther, "Preface to the New Testament," *The Spirit of the Protestant Reformation*, ed. and trans. Bertram Lee Woolf ("The Reformation Writings of Martin Luther," Vol. II; London: Lutterworth, 1956), p. 282.
17. H. Richard Niebuhr, *Responsible Self*, p. 78.
18. Reinhold Niebuhr, *Destiny*, pp. 94-95.
19. Barth, IV/2, 745; IV/1, 17; III/4, 116-17, 341.
20. Luke 10:31-35.
21. Luther, *Galatians 1-4*, p. 44; Calvin, *Institutes*, iii.19, 7.
22. Bultmann, *Existence and Faith*, p. 217; Luther, *Galatians 5-6*, p. 117.
23. Luke 15:11-32.
24. Reinhold Niebuhr, *Destiny*, pp. 196-97.
25. H. Richard Niebuhr, *Responsible Self*, p. 61.
26. Bultmann, *Existence and Faith*, p. 56.
27. Barth, III/2, 261.
28. Calvin, *Institutes*, ii.4, 14.
29. Bonhoeffer, *Letters and Papers*, p. 113.
30. Bultmann, *Existence and Faith*, p. 56.
31. Mark 6:14-27.
32. Bonhoeffer, *Ethics*, pp. 197-98.
33. Tillich, *Protestant Era*, p. 133.
34. Bonhoeffer, *Ethics*, pp. 179-80; Barth, IV/2, 93.
35. Barth, IV/2, 473, 531; Calvin, *Institutes*, iii.19, 4, and iv.10, 11; Reinhold Niebuhr, *Destiny*, pp. 11-13.

36. Calvin, *Institutes*, iv.10, 10; Schleiermacher, *On Religion*, p. 59.

37. Tillich, *Courage to Be*, pp. 49-50; Bultmann, *Essays*, p. 7; Barth, IV/2, 531.

38. Calvin, *Institutes*, ii.4, 14; Bultmann, *Essays*, p. 44.

39. Bonhoeffer, *Ethics*, pp. 226, 237.

40. Tillich, *Systematic Theology*, III, 232; Reinhold Niebuhr, *Nature*, p. 256; Luther, *Galatians 5-6*, pp. 8, 13; cf. *Galatians 1-4*, pp. 70, 404-5; Tillich, *Protestant Era*, p. 146; *Shaking of the Foundations*, p. 170.

41. Reinhold Niebuhr, *Interpretation*, p. 14.

42. Calvin, *Institutes*, iii.19, 8, and 4, 10, 23.

43. Calvin, *Institutes*, iii.19, 7.

44. Luther, *Galatians 5-6*, p. 13; "Freedom of a Christian," p. 368.

45. Barth, IV/2, 473; Reinhold Niebuhr, *Destiny*, pp. 320-21; Luther, *Galatians 1-4*, 404-5.

46. Matt. 23:23-24.

47. Tillich, *Shaking of the Foundations*, p. 159; Luther, "Freedom of a Christian," p. 367; cf. *Galatians 1-4*, p. 133.

48. Bonhoeffer, *Ethics*, pp. 327-28; cf. *Letters and Papers*, p. 106.

49. Reinhold Niebuhr, *Interpretation*, p. 14.

50. *Bultmann, Essays*, pp. 140-41; Reinhold Niebuhr, *Interpretation*, p. 48; Barth, III/4, 673.

51. Bultmann, *Essays*, p. 60.

52. H. Richard Niebuhr, *Responsible Self*, p. 116.

53. Matt. 23:5, 25-28.

54. Bultmann, *Existence and Faith*, pp. 181-82, 255; *Essays*, pp. 60, 140-41.

55. Mark 6:14-29.

56. H. Richard Niebuhr, *Responsible Self*, p. 116.

57. Reinhold Niebuhr, *Nature*, p. 272; Barth, III/2, 261; III/4, 500-501; Bonhoeffer, *Ethics*, p. 213; Luther, "Freedom of a Christian," p. 365; Kierkegaard, *Training in Christianity*, p. 71.

58. Tillich, *Systematic Theology*, III, 232.

59. Bultmann, *Existence and Faith*, p. 255.

60. H. Richard Niebuhr, *Responsible Self*, p. 61; Bonhoeffer, *Ethics*, pp. 197-98.

61. Bonhoeffer, *Letters and Papers*, pp. 222-23.

62. Luther, *Galatians 1-4*, pp. 404-5.

63. Barth, IV/1, 345; IV/2, 93.

64. Bultmann, *Essays*, p. 60; Calvin, *Institutes*, iii.19, 8; Tillich, *Shaking of the Foundations*, p. 170.

65. Kierkegaard, *Postscript*, p. 121.

66. Duncombe, "The Evaluation of University Covenant Communities."

67. Elizabeth L. Wesley, "Perseverative Behavior in a Concept Formation Task as a Function of Manifest Anxiety and Rigidity," *Journal of Abnormal and Social Psychology*, XLVIII (1953), 129-34.

68. *Ibid.*, p. 129.

69. T. W. Adorno, *et al.*, *The Authoritarian Personality* (New York: Harper, 1950).

70. Abraham S. Luchins, "The Einstellung Test of Rigidity: Its Relation

to Concreteness of Thinking," *Journal of Consulting Psychology*, XV (1951), 303-10.

71. Leonard H. Ainsworth, "Rigidity, Insecurity, and Stress," *Journal of Abnormal and Social Psychology*, LVI (1958), 67-74.

72. Wesley, "Perseverative Behavior in a Concept Formation Task," pp. 129-34.

73. Gardner, "Cognitive Control," pp. 1-185.

74. Frenkel-Brunswik, "Intolerance of Ambiguity as an Emotional and Perceptual Personality Variable," pp. 108-43.

75. The interpretative theory supporting the use of these problem-solving tests is discussed in greater detail in the following chapter (pp. 183-87).

76. Millon, "Authoritarianism, Intolerance of Ambiguity, and Rigidity Under Ego- and Task-involving Conditions," pp. 29-33.

77. James E. Dittes and Harold H. Kelly, "Effects of Different Conditions of Acceptance upon Conformity to Group Norms," *Journal of Abnormal and Social Psychology*, LIII (1956), 100-107.

78. John McDavid, "Personality and Situational Determinants of Conformity," *Journal of Abnormal and Social Psychology*, LVIII (1959), 241-46; "Personality Correlates with Two Kinds of Conforming Behavior," *Journal of Personality*, XXXII (1964), 420-35.

79. Leon Festinger, *A Theory of Cognitive Dissonance* (Evanston, Ill.: Row, Peterson, 1957).

80. Jack W. Brehm and Arthur R. Cohen, *Explorations in Cognitive Dissonance* (New York: Wiley, 1962).

---

chapter VII

THE NECESSITY AND RISKS
OF BEHAVIORAL THEOLOGY

I

Questioning Is Not Enough

We live at a time of radical questioning. For Christians this means a searching appraisal of many settled areas of Christian life and belief. An Anglican bishop is questioning our traditional concepts of God, an Episcopal bishop is disputing the Trinity and the divinity of Jesus, and other Christian theologians are prying up the very stones upon which the church has rested for centuries. The situation is viewed with alarm by many sincere Christians, but their protest will not hold back the tide. Christian orthodoxy is being swept away.

Similar observations have led many to conclude that the death of orthodoxy means the end of the institutional church. This may be so. But it also may be true that the churches are on the brink of a new era. That which appears to be dangerously undermining the walls of the institutional

---

church may be laying bedrock foundations for a far more durable structure.

One thing seems certain, however—to survive this age of questioning, institutional Christianity must do more than toy with the idea of honesty. The rash of recent books on honesty in the church illustrates this concern but falls short of specifying the conditions under which honesty is a real possibility for a local church. What good does it do to honestly question a claim such as "Church-going is *good* for you" without a means of honestly deciding the truth or falsity of the claim? There is no course of action appropriate to merely raising the issue. Churchmen will either quit the church or continue on as before, with little justification for either course of action. In the absence of reliable knowledge to the contrary, such radical questioning may merely provide the occasion for Christians to act upon their private inclinations. Radical questioning can be the first step either toward honesty or toward greater self-deception.

If it is a step toward honesty, it must enable an honest judgment. The minimal prerequisite for making *any* judgment—including the judgment that no judgment is possible —about the effect of the institutional church on Christian life is a clearer notion of what it means to be a mature Christian. If nowhere else, one would think such clarity would exist in the minds of the great contemporary theologians. Yet is seems doubtful that even as brilliant a church theologian as Karl Barth could have positively identified a mature Christian. This is not to suggest that sound theology has little to do with the making of this kind of judgment. Without it the task would be impossible. But neither does it follow that Christian theology itself provides a ready-made method for distinguishing a mature Christian from a clever imitation. A significant gap has always existed between the conceptual clarity of the best Christian theology and the empirical clarity required for reliable judgments among persons. It has been the aim of these chapters to help close this gap.

II

The Quest for Criteria of Christian Maturity

There is nothing novel about this aim. Christianity has been searching for reliable bench marks since the beginning. Whether as occasional checks against errors in judgment or as the basis of judgment itself, Christians have continually sought objective criteria for identifying living instances of mature Christian life. The story is long and cannot be recounted here. But certainly no proposal for a different set of bench marks should be considered without at least mentioning a few of the more important traditional criteria and giving some indication of why they would prove less than satisfactory for twentieth-century Christianity.

Early Virtues, Signs, and Marks

The complex system of Christian virtues, elaborated and formalized by the Christian church during its first millennium, was initially rooted in practice and belief recorded in the New Testament. Perhaps the most complete catalog of these virtues is given in Gal. 5:19-23, where fifteen "works of the flesh" are contrasted with nine "fruit[s] of the Spirit." From this and other sources[1] evolved the "theological," the "moral," the "natural," the "supernatural," and other virtues. Since Reformation times, at least in Protestant circles, the virtues have suffered as a result of their unfortunate association with medieval moralism and "works-righteousness." But there seems little doubt that for many early churchmen the virtues provided a humanizing yardstick against the less scripturally oriented standards of institutionalized Christianity.

As criteria for mature Christian life, however, the virtues have a number of limitations. In the first place, it is not always clear how even those virtues taken directly from scripture can be legitimately justified by scripture in larger context. Then there is the problem of their static nature. A virtue appropriate for one situation might not be for another, as Jesus illustrated repeatedly. Nor do the virtues evidence a feel for the process of personal and corporate development which requires a comparative and not an absolute measure. For example, it is reasonable to expect that spiritual growth may often demand a temporary regression from a previously higher level of achieved virtue. Then comes the inevitable difficulty of interpreting feigned from true virtue, especially if the former is habitually and not willfully intended.[2] Finally, there is the confusion over which and/or how many virtues are necessary for establishing the presence of the Spirit and in what comparative degree of perfection and duration.

Related to the virtues was a system of various "marks" and "signs" of the church. Since the primary intent was that of distinguishing a true church from a false one—and not a true Christian from a false one—it often happened that such marks or signs referred to institutional practices and beliefs and not to individual or group characteristics. This is true of the reformers as well, although they undertook to guard their *notae ecclesiae* of word and sacrament by various other signs. Chief among these was the stipulation that the marks were of no avail unless the congregation itself was characterized by a "lively faith" in Christ and the "good works" that flow from such faith.

While most of the traditional marks of the church are means and not ends of the Christian life (miracles and holiness being recurrent exceptions), the Protestant signs probably show a greater degree of insight into the spiritual workings of the Christian community. Luther's understanding of these signs allows for more flexibility and depth of application than that found in the medieval system of virtues. But, unfortunately, the particular quality of inwardness he describes as necessary to the Christian life did not permit unambiguous identification from without—and as his later life evidences, sometimes not from within as well. True, both he and Calvin expected that good works would flow naturally from such a state of spiritual life, but these works were apt to be as deceptive to the observer as the quality of inwardness could be to the experiencer.

Modern "Secular" Approaches

In recent times church sociologists have made a fresh approach to the problem of establishing objective criteria for the Christian life. Perhaps the most popular technique is that of giving concrete contemporary meaning to various models or images of the church found in biblical and theological literature and then noting the amount of discrepancy between these churchly ideals and actual churches. For example, from the body-of-Christ image can be deduced an economically, socially, and racially integrated church. An objective measure of integration is then applied to a particular church and the result interpreted as evidence for or against that church's implicit claim to be a true church of Christ. Likewise, any number of "mission" models have been drawn into service on the assumption that when a community of persons takes deliberate and effective ethical action beyond its own sphere, a good deal of what it does will be both visible and measurable.

While this brief description fails to do justice to the variety or sophistication of sociological approaches, there are some serious questions to be raised. In the first place, it is not at all clear that their commonly used models and images are broad enough for an adequate definition of the church or Christian life—especially when only one or two models are used. Then there is the question of their translation into contemporary form. Theologians might argue, for instance, that racial segregation is not necessarily antithetical to the body-of-Christ image or that an instance of segregation does not constitute prima facie evidence against spiritual life irrespective of other situational factors. In short, it would seem that many of the same limitations plaguing the use of the virtues, marks, and signs pop up again in the interpretive stage of the modern sociological studies. By their use of modern research designs and statistical methods, church sociologists have made a significant contribution to our knowledge of the institutional church and those who call themselves Christians. But the question remains whether such data permit theologically valid inferences concerning the nature of the church and Christian life.

Another Holy Grail?

Without the ability to concretely identify mature Christian life, genuine Christian growth, an effective Christian method, and a true Christian church, Christianity is in trouble. That trouble is boiling to the surface in the form of practical questions that cannot now be answered, questions such as, "Why should I go to church?" If Christianity has been less than honest by presuming to answer such questions, it has not been inwardly unaware of the problem. Christian history reveals repeated attempts to find a viable method to detect or ensure the workings of the Spirit in the life of man. As the various cited examples suggest, these attempts have largely failed because the church has confused Christian ends with churchly means or has adopted theologically and empirically questionable methods of identifying Christian ends.

But have we offered a better alternative in these pages? To pretend that this approach is without significant limitations would be unrealistic. Perhaps all that may be said with certainty is that we can know a little more about these limitations and whether they can be removed. Someday we may know more. This is the advantage that comes with basing an approach upon empirically verifiable knowledge. Already in the preceding chapters many questions have been raised with the reliability of our own data and the adequacy of the inferences used to apply them to the Protestant image of mature humanity. But these questions have for the most part dealt with specifics. There are also legitimate questions to be brought touching the very foundations upon which such an undertaking rests. How is it possible to empiricize theology without diluting its essence? Can we even speak of "Christian" maturity without mentioning Christ or one's belief in him? Are tests and measures reliable enough today, even by their own standards? These are the real concerns that give us pause. It is time that they were considered.

III

Theology's Behavorial Implications

In broadest scope this book represents an attempt to bring together two established disciplines, theology and personality testing, in a limited but systematic way in order to give empirical expression to a sector of Protestant thought. Theologically stated, the possibilities explored by this book arise from the conviction in Protestant thought that God's work among men is nothing less than the restoration of full humanity. Mature Christian life is a fruit of this work not because it adds an invisible or indefinable spiritual "something" to human existence, but because it allows man to be the person God intended. Whatever else this may mean, it cannot mean less than the freedom for full use of the human faculties.

If this "less than" permits a theologically related meaning to be attached to certain empirical operations, there is a "more than" which limits the degree of correspondence possible. Theology speaks of that which has more than logical or empirical significance. The temptation to reduce theology to a set of empirical operations is not unlike the temptation to reduce it to a set of ethical principles. The fact that these operations or principles may be implied by certain theolological assertions does not grant the right to separate the assertions from the total theological context that gives them meaning. Too great a haste to distill the empirical essence of theology can compromise the integrity of both disciplines.

Unfortunately, the chief offender has often been a simplistic "behavioral" interpretation of theology. A behavioral understanding of theology, such as proposed in this book, need not be insensitive and heavy-handed. In fact there is good reason to believe that Protestant theology must be understood behaviorally before it is adequately understood theoretically. Reflection on the nature of human behavior shows why this is so.

Theology's Behavioral Roots

Nothing is more humanly interesting to us than human behavior. Our thoughts and conversations are largely about human behavior. The vast majority of our reading materials —whether newspapers, comic books, textbooks, or novels— concerns human behavior. We are forever examining it, describing it, and explaining it in ourselves and in others.

Whether we ever undertake the formal study of human behavior within an academic or practical discipline, we are all students of human behavior by virtue of being human.

It is sometimes forgotten that Christian theologians are human too. These men who fill our minds with staggering concepts and profound ideas are behaving humans like the rest of us. They have been involved in human drama since infancy and have a consuming interest in it. It is largely this interest that has drawn them to theology, for here the human drama takes on eternal significance. This is not to suggest that their views of things not temporal are only reflections of the human scene in disguise. It is merely to affirm that theologians are first and foremost students of human behavior and that their theology has human significance. Obvious as this may be, were it not so, no better way for identifying mature Christian life could be proposed.

When the theologian thinks about mature Christian life, it may not be in what *he* would call behavioral terms. For instance, he may conceive of the Christian as one who loves God, believes in Jesus Christ, has faith, etc. Pressed on what he means, the theologian is likely to claim that such terms are unique to Christian experience (i.e., only the experiencer can understand the experience) and refer to inward events having no *necessary* outward and observable expression. The answer is correct as far as it goes. The difficulty is that it tempts the unwarranted inference that the mature Christian life cannot be understood or identified in different behavioral terms.

However unique or inward an experience, it nevertheless implies certain behavioral expectations. For example, "to have faith" implies that in any given situation certain behaviors are appropriate and others are not. This is not the same as saying that certain behaviors necessarily follow from faith regardless of circumstance. It means that under one set of circumstances "to have faith" implies behaviors of one sort, and under another set of circumstances "to have faith" implies behavior of a different sort. To be able to specify which behaviors are expected of the mature Christian and which are not is the first step in identifying him.

Why certain behavioral expectations are implied by such theological terms should be no mystery. It is the way these terms come to have meaning for the theologian. Where else are they rooted if not in the complex of behavioral events that make up the life experience of the theologian himself? Human behavior is his primary experience, his first language, his most consuming interest. As a theologian he does not transcend behavior, but draws upon it to express what is unique, inward, and most characteristic of the Christian life.

Consider the theologian as a human, involved in the process of human growth. As he observes himself and others in social activity, he comes to associate certain behavioral sequences (under certain conditions) with a particular inward experience or set of related experiences having a unique emotional significance for him. He seeks to understand these inward experiences in terms of the outward events that elicit them, if for no other reason than to gain some measure of control over them. Thus over the years he learns to expect that an otherwise inexpressible inner experience will more likely follow from some behavioral sequences than others. Although he may not be consciously aware of this learning process, he participates in the human drama on the basis of it.

In the same way that these outer experiences give rise to inner experience, so does the growing complex of inner experiences find symbolic expression in the language of theology. It is the theologian's way of organizing, understanding, and controlling his legacy of behavior-associated feelings convictions, attitudes, and other inward events of importance. Through symbolic expression the theologian draws on the experience of others to enrich and extend his understanding of mature Christian life. What has been done, said, and thought by Jesus and Paul—and by Christians and theologians down through the ages—is appropriated as part of his own experience. It helps further to sort out what is "Christian" and what is not in terms of his own inward experience and related behavioral events.

This is why we can speak of theological descriptions as implying behavioral expectations, no matter how symbolic and abstract the description. The theologian is acutely aware of the connection between these theological descriptions and the complex inward experiences they reflect. For him, phrases like "to have faith" have largely come to *mean* these unique and inward experiences. He is less conscious of their behavioral correlates. For all his native skill in observing and interpreting human behavior, the theologian has tended to ignore the obvious fact that it is just these inward experiences as they are symbolized theologically which relate his own behavioral observations to his own behavioral expectations. By focusing on the symbolic connection between these two behavioral aspects of the human drama, the very heart of Protestant thought about the Christian man can be used to identify the Christian man.

Beginnings of a Behavioral Theology

Not all theology is unaware of its behavioral implications. Much of the liberal, pragmatic, and empirical theology of the late nineteenth and early twentieth centuries sought to specify the behaviors of the Christian personality. While there is much to be learned from this theology, it is marred by two shortcomings. One is its partiality for certain doctrinal themes at the expense of others. For this reason little attempt is made to specify the behavioral implications of many central Christian doctrines. A second shortcoming is its static, moralistic cast. Christian behaviors are often little more than medieval Christian virtues in modern setting. Emphasis is placed on the act itself, not on the ability to perform the act and the warranting circumstances.

Of more importance, perhaps, is the fact that even traditional Protestant thought does not totally ignore its behavioral implications. Nearly every prominent Protestant theologian read today has at one time or other done a treatise, book, or section of a systematic theology on Christian behavior. Such topical treatments of the Christian man, Christian freedom, the life of faith, sanctification, etc., can be extremely helpful, especially when they reveal a sensitive awareness of human dynamics. But Protestant theologians are often most instructive when making offhand comments in other contexts. Who has not read Luther on the Incarnation or Atonement, for example, without being brought up short by a particularly arresting illustration of Christian behavior? Sometimes these occur in explicit asides, homilies, or comparisons. Other times the associative link is the reader's. However it occurs, there is a genuine theological insight in which behavioral expectations are clarified.

As long as it is necessary to infer the validity of empirical operations from theological assertions of broader intent, however, the possibilities for significant contributions in this area will be limited. Theologians themselves must be involved in the search for individual and social expressions of mature Christian life having empirically identifiable form. This means the ability and willingness to specify the discernible conditions of renewal in the Spirit. The risk of a new casuistry is probably no greater than the risk of continued ambivalence with respect to confirming and disconfirming events. A theology which does not actively pursue knowledge of the concrete instances of God's redeeming work among men may find itself speaking with continually less knowledge of things having more than empirical significance.

IV

Are the Tests That Good?

The field of personality research has yet to come of age. It is still struggling under the effects of unrealistically simple concepts, models, and methods found useful in its childhood. During the past fifteen years there has been a bursting of the old forms. Preoccupation with various traditional categories of behavior, characteristics, and surface traits has given way increasingly to an interest in the identification and description of underlying variables or genotypes. The general effect has been to fragment once related areas of research and to initiate a search for a new integrating principle.

Abelson[3] has observed that while the past few years have produced an "enormous accumulation of little bits of evidence," two lines of progress can be delineated. The first is the development of more effective laboratory manipulations "so that a wide range of social situations can be created in a controlled environment." The second is the increased quality and quantity of personality assessment devices being developed for the more comprehensive computer-analyzed studies. Given a reasonable projection of these lines of current progress, the measures described in this book may not need to bear the major burden of empirical identification in years to come.

At present the major weakness of personality research may be, as Holzman[4] suggests, "the swamping effect of overriding method variance" caused by the lack of uniform concepts, method, and results. For example, it is not often that the same research design holds the interest of experimenters long enough to produce the patterning of replications which logically eliminate all alternative explanations. Such factors as age, sex, culture, and socio-economic class are not systematically varied in the selection of subjects. With rare exceptions the validity of most measures discussed in this book could not extend beyond American college-age populations without additional testing.

But How Can This Test Have Theological Meaning?

Most often a reader's uneasiness with empirical measures goes deeper. Let's look at a specific example. A prominent theologian, upon reading the preceding description of the Einstellung test (pp. 161-62), raised the following objection:

I know a high school girl who is a whiz at that kind of test. She's way up at the top in the SAT scores in mathematical aptitude, and she knocks the top out of lesser tests. On verbal tests she's good but not exceptional. At games of the Einstellung type she can't find anybody who will play with her, and competitors simply bore her. I can not be persuaded that her attendance at Sunday school and church has anything to do with her high "indicators." The author sees this when he notes that a high I.Q. may help on the Einstellung test. But the correctors he then proposes all (as it seems to me) rely upon some peculiar aptitude. That church-going has much to do with the result seems incredible.

The theologian is rightly suspicious of problem-solving tests that can indicate *more* than the personality characteristics in question. The task is to eliminate the "more." He senses—rightly or wrongly—that this high school girl is scoring high on Einstellung type tests because of factors other than Christian maturity. What else could be accounting for her superior performance? I.Q.? This can be controlled by administering a standard I.Q. test. Practice or experience in doing these tests? This is certainly more difficult to control. Here it is often necessary to concurrently administer other "rigidity" or "perseveration" measures based on an entirely different principle, such as the dog-to-cat picture book or the even less consciously mediated autokinetic effect. If the Einstellung *plus* the supportive indicators shows the same results, not only is the practice effect ruled out, but the Einstellung scores further strengthen the reliability of the dog-to-cat and autokinetic results. It is the package of consistent results and not the lone test or measure that deserves confidence.

But the theologian is still uneasy. He can imagine this high school girl turning in superior scores on the basis of "some peculiar aptitude." We all know people who seem to have a knack or aptitude for doing things—carrying a tune, making sensible decisions, writing poetry, fixing things. Beyond I.Q. and practice this may reflect a greater interest or enjoyment or even some subtle physical ability. The list might be endless—and certainly the thought of some yet undiscovered factor seriously "contaminating" the results of any test makes humble men of researchers.

But over the years a number of these factors have at least been teased out and identified. Some are found well controlled. If the interest or enjoyment factor worries the theologian, for example, he will find that significant differences in interest and enjoyment can be effectively neutralized in most high-pressure testing situations (like the Einstellung) given under ego-involving instructions. Physical aptitude undoubtedly plays a part in tasks requiring body coordination and agility but seems as unlikely as bad breath or green toenail polish to affect the girl's Einstellung performance.

Yet the possibility remains. Computer analysis may someday turn up just such a cause of high scores on Einstellung tests whether or not we have a theory to explain why. The odds favoring the existence of unknown causal factors are good, but the odds are infinitesimally small that such factors have an effect strong enough to make an essentially constricted girl appear free and flexible—or vice-versa.

More likely the theologian's "peculiar aptitude" is a composite of those qualities of adequate response that the Einstellung test identifies. Aptitudes not easily parceled out, labeled, and controlled, have deep roots in the very personality structures most sensitive to a person's fundmental sense of security. It would be strange indeed if truly basic aptitudes were somehow exempted from the work of the Spirit.

And the Church?

The theologian concluded, "That church-going has much to do with the result seems incredible." It seems incredible to the writer as well; he must bear at least partial responsibility for this common misunderstanding. The book begins with a problem facing the church: to minister effectively it must know who is a mature Christian and who is not. The five central chapters are offered as a solution to the problem. But no practical parish program based on the polar personality profiles and supporting empirical measures is proposed. That is left to the reader. If you now are better able, by virtue of this book, to see where the redeeming work of God is taking place, you can judge where Christian growth is occurring within your congregation. If it is not occurring, experiment with other approaches until you find something that begins moving significant parts of your congregation toward the "mature Christian" end of the spectrum. Whatever that new approach—whether exegetical preaching fifty-two Sundays a year or marihuana parties for the altar guild—it is better than what you had for the simple reason that it works.

There is no intention, then, to claim that church-going causes higher Einstellung scores. Church-going may very well cause lower scores or have no effect at all. It all depends upon what is going on in the church. What is being claimed is that Protestant thought describes the effects of God's redeeming grace in the lives of people in a way that reflects, among other things, the response behavior identified by these types of problem-solving tests. Or to put it another way, *if* these theologians are correct and *if* this girl's church or Sunday school is a significant source of God's grace for her life, *then* we can expect that her performance on adequately controlled tests such as these will be significantly better than had she not attended church or Sunday school— or better than the performance of her peers, everything being equal, who do not have similar sources of grace at work in their lives.

V

New Directions

There is some indication that one focus of future research may be in the area of the yet largely undefined relationship between stress, threat, ego-involvement, ambiguity, and insecurity. The rough synthesis of these conditions described in Chapter II is based more upon conceptual relationships in psychoanalytic theory and theology than on a clearly demonstrated pattern of empirical relationships. Specifically, that which constitutes the connection between a basic sense of security and tolerance of ambiguity has only been suggested by a scattering of correlations. These concepts should receive more precise and situationally varied operational definition since they may well turn out to be the key to a new organizing principle or "general factor" in personality research.

In final perspective, this book has mainly a heuristic value. A major emphasis has been that of pointing beyond the various correspondences shown to indications of that which cannot yet be shown: a theological motif that cannot be reduced to a set of assertions but that "speaks to" the situation of the subject as he struggles with a task, or a particularly ingenious means of simulating reality or tapping theologically related behavior that lacks the necessary controls or sophistication of design to qualify as an adequate measure. These do not permit an informed judgment, but they indicate something of the general basis upon which a more reliable distinction between persons could be made were this to become a major area of concern for both theologians and those in personality research.

There is also a note of urgency in this. At a time when the Christian ministry itself has begun to look beyond theology for direction and authority, there is a suggestion that the meaning and usefulness of theology may become increasingly limited unless theology is grounded in identifiable experience. General references to man or existence, having little possibility for concrete confirmation of disconfirmation, are not sufficient. A theology which begins by pointing definitively to "this Man" among all others implies the ability to point definitely to "that man" among all others. As long as "that man" remains identifiably no man, there may be little reason to expect that we can speak more definitively of "this Man."

NOTES

1. Matt. 5; 12:33-35; Luke 6:43-45; John 15:1-17; I Cor. 13.
2. The predominantly unconscious processes of compensation and re-action formation can often deceive both the subject and his observers.
3. Robert P. Abelson, "Commentary: Situational Variables in Personality Research," *Measurement in Personality and Cognition*, ed. Samuel Messick and John Ross (New York: Wiley, 1962), p. 241.
4. Wayne H. Holzman, "Personality Structure," *Annual Review of Psychology*, XVI (1965), 150-51.

BIBLIOGRAPHY

I. Theology

Barth, Karl. *Church Dogmatics*. Vol. III/2. Ed. G. W. Bromiley and T. F. Torrance. Trans. G. W. Bromiley *et al.* Edinburgh: T. & T. Clark, 1960.

————. *Church Dogmatics*. Vol. III/4. Ed. G. W. Bromiley and T. F. Torrance. Trans. A. T. Mackay *et al.* Edinburgh: T. & T. Clark, 1961.

————. *Church Dogmatics*. Vol. IV/1. Ed. G. W. Bromiley and T. F. Torrance. Trans. G. W. Bromiley. Edinburgh: T. & T. Clark, 1956.

————. *Church Dogmatics*. Vol. IV/2. Ed. G. W. Bromiley and T. F. Torrance. Trans. G. W. Bromiley. Edinburgh: T. & T. Clark, 1958.

————. *Church Dogmatics*. Vol. IV/3(1). Ed. G. W. Bromiley and T. F. Torrance. Trans. G. W. Bromiley. Edinburgh: T. & T. Clark, 1961.

————. *Church Dogmatics*. Vol. IV/3(2). Ed. G. W. Bromiley and T. F. Torrance. Trans. G. W. Bromiley. Edinburgh: T. & T. Clark, 1962.

Bonhoeffer, Dietrich. *The Cost of Discipleship*. Trans. R. H. Fuller. Rev. ed.; New York: Macmillan 1959.

————. *Ethics.* Ed. Eberhard Bethge. Trans. Neville H. Smith. New York: Macmillan, 1955.

————. *Letters and Papers from Prison.* Ed. Eberhard Bethge. Trans. R. H. Fuller. New York: Macmillan, 1953.

————. *Life Together.* Trans. John W. Doberstein. New York: Harper, 1954.

Bultmann, Rudolf. *Essays: Philosophical and Theological.* Trans. James C. G. Greig. New York: Macmillan, 1955.

————. *Existence and Faith: Shorter Writings of Rudolf Bultmann.* Trans. Shubert M. Ogden. Meridian Books; Cleveland: World, 1960.

————. *Jesus Christ and Mythology.* New York: Scribner's, 1958.

————. *Primitive Christianity in Its Comtemporary Setting.* Trans. R. H. Fuller. Meridian Books; Cleveland: World, 1956.

Bultmann, Rudolf, *et al.* *Kerygma and Myth: A Theological Debate.* Ed. Hans W. Bartsch. Trans. R. H. Fuller. Rev. ed.; New York: Harper, 1961.

Calvin, John. *Calvin: Commentaries.* Ed. and trans. Joseph Haroutunian and Louise P. Smith. ("Library of Christian Classics," Vol. XXIII.) Philadelphia: Westminster, 1958.

————. *Institutes of the Christian Religion.* Trans. Henry Beveridge. 2 vols. Grand Rapids: Eerdmans, 1962.

Kierkegaard, Søren. *Concluding Unscientific Postscript to the Philosophical Fragments.* Trans. David F. Swenson and Walter Lowrie. Princeton: Princeton University Press, 1941.

————. *Fear and Trembling and the Sickness unto Death.* Trans. Walter Lowrie. Garden City, N. Y.: Doubleday, 1954.

————. *For Self-examination.* Trans. Edna Hong and Howard Hong. Minneapolis: Augsburg, 1940.

————. *Philosophical Fragments or a Fragment of Philosophy.* Trans. David F. Swenson. Princeton: Princeton University Press, 1936.

————. *Training in Christianity and the Edifying Discourse Which Accompanied It.* Trans. Walter Lowrie. London: Oxford University Press, 1941.

————. *Works of Love.* Trans. David F. Swenson and Lillian M. Swenson. Princeton: Princeton University Press, 1946.

Luther, Martin. "The Freedom of a Christian." Trans. W. A. Lambert. *Career of the Reformer: I.* Ed. Harold J. Grimm. ("Luther's Works," Vol. XXXI.) Philadelphia: Muhlenburg, 1957. Pp. 333-77.

————. *Lectures on Galatians 1535, Chapters 1-4.* Ed. and trans. Jaroslav Pelikan. ("Luther's Works," Vol. XXVI.) St. Louis: Concordia, 1963.

————. *Lectures on Galatians 1535, Chapters 5-6.* Trans. Jaroslav Pelikan. *Lectures on Galatians 1519, Chapters 1-6.* Trans. Richard

Jungkuntz. Ed. Jaroslav Pelikan. ("Luther's Works," Vol. XXVII.) St. Louis: Concordia, 1964.

————. *Lectures on Romans.* Ed. and trans. Wilhelm Pauck, ("Library of Christian Classics," Vol. XV.) Philadelphia: Westminster, 1961.

————. "Preface to the Book of Psalms," *The Spirit of the Protestant Reformation.* Ed. and trans. Bertram Lee Woolf. ("The Reformation Writings of Martin Luther," Vol. II.) London: Lutterworth, 1956. Pp. 267-71.

————. "Preface to the Epistle of St. Paul to the Romans," *The Spirit of the Protestant Reformation.* Ed. and trans. Bertram Lee Woolf. ("The Reformation Writings of Martin Luther," Vol. II.) London: Lutterworth, 1956. Pp. 284-300.

————. "Preface to the New Testament," *The Spirit of the Protestant Reformation.* Ed. and trans. Bertram Lee Woolf. ("The Reformation Writings of Martin Luther," Vol. II) London: Lutterworth, 1956. Pp. 278-83.

————. "Two Kinds of Righteousness." Trans. Lowell J. Satre. *Career of the Reformer: I.* Ed. Harold J. Grimm. ("Luther's Works," Vol. XXXI.) Philadelphia: Muhlenburg, 1957. Pp. 293-306.

Machen, J. Gresham. *Christianity and Liberalism.* New York: Macmillan, 1923.

Niebuhr, H. Richard. *Christ and Culture.* New York: Harper, 1951.

————. *The Meaning of Revelation.* New York: Macmillan, 1960.

————. *The Purpose of the Church and Its Ministry.* In collaboration with Daniel Day Williams and James M. Gustafson. New York: Harper, 1956.

————. *Radical Monotheism and Western Culture.* New York: Harper, 1957.

————. *The Responsible Self.* New York: Harper, 1963.

Niebuhr, Reinhold. *An Interpretation of Christian Ethics.* Meridian Books; Cleveland: World, 1956.

————. *The Nature and Destiny of Man.* 2 vols. New York: Scribner's, 1964.

Schleiermacher, Friedrich. *The Christian Faith.* Ed. H. R. Mackintosh and J. S. Stewart. Edinburg: T. & T. Clark, 1928.

————. *On Religion: Speeches to Its Cultured Despisers.* Trans. John Oman. New York: Harper, 1958.

Tillich, Paul. *The Courage to Be.* New Haven: Yale University Press, 1952.

————. *Dynamics of Faith.* New York: Harper, 1957.

————. *The Protestant Era.* Trans. James L. Adams. Abridged ed. Chicago: University of Chicago Press, 1957.

————. *The Shaking of the Foundations.* New York: Scribner's 1948.

————. *Systematic Theology.* Vol. III. Chicago: University of Chicago Press, 1963.

II. Empirical Studies

The titles of some journals are abbreviated as follows: *JASP, Journal of Abnormal and Social Psychology; JCP, Journal of Consulting Psychology; JP, Journal of Personality.*

Abelson, Robert P. "Commentary: Situational Variables in Personality Research," *Measurement in Personality and Cognition.* Ed. Samuel Messick and John Ross. New York: Wiley, 1962. Pp. 241-48.

Adorono, T. W., *et al. The Authoritarian Personality.* New York: Harper, 1950.

Ainsworth, Leonard H. "Rigidity, Insecurity, and Stress," *JASP*, LVI (1958), 67-74.

Ainsworth, Leonard H., and Ainsworth, Mary D. *Measuring Security in Personal Adjustment.* Toronto: University of Toronto Press, 1958.

Becker, Wesley C. "Perceptual Rigidity as Measured by Aniseikonic Lenses," *JASP*, XLIX (1954), 419-22.

Belenky, Robert L. "The Relationship Between Accuracy in Self-perception and the Perception of Others: A Study of Estimates of Performance on a Test of Values and a Test of Aspiration Level," *Dissertation Abstracts*, XX (1960), 3825-26.

Blum, Gerald S. "Perceptual Defense Revisited," *JASP*, LI (1955), 24-29.

Bossom, Joseph, and Maslow, A. H. "Security of Judges as a Factor in Impressions of Warmth in Others," *JASP*, LV (1957), 147-48.

Brehm, Jack W., and Cohen, Arthur R. *Explorations in Cognitive Dissonance.* New York: Wiley, 1962.

Bronfenbrenner, Urie, *et al.* "The Analysis of Social Sensitivity (Sympathy)," *American Psychologist*, VII (1952), 324.

Bruninga, C. L., *et al.* "Some Effects of Pastoral Visitation with Mental Patients." Norwich, Conn.: Norwich State Hospital, 1967.

Budner, Stanley. "Intolerance of Ambiguity as a Personality Variable," *JP*, XXX (1962), 29-50.

Cartwright, Desmond S. "Self-consistency as a Factor Affecting Immediate Recall," *JASP*, LII (1956), 212-18.

Cline, Victor B., and Richards, James M., Jr. "Accuracy of Interpersonal Perception—a General Trait?" *JASP*, LX (1960), 1-8.

Cottrell, Nickolas B. "The Measurement of Unwarranted Self-evaluative Behavior," *Dissertation Abstracts*, XXV (1964), 1378.

Cronbach, Lee J. *Essentials of Psychological Testing.* 2nd ed. New York: Harper, 1960.

D'Amato, M. R., and Gumenik, W. E. "Some Effects of Immediate Versus Delayed Shock on an Instrumental Response and Cognitive Processes," *JASP,* LX (1960), 64-67.

Deutsch, Morton. "Trust, Trustworthiness, and the F-Scale," *JASP,* LXI (1960), 138-40.

Dittes, James E. "Effect of Changes in Self-esteem upon Impulsiveness and Deliberation in Making Judgments," *JASP,* LVIII (1959), 348-56.

———. "Impulsive Closure as Reaction to Failure-induced Threat," *JASP,* LXIII (1961), 562-69.

Dittes, James E., and Kelly, Harold H. "Effects of Different Conditions of Acceptance upon Conformity to Group Norms," *JASP,* LIII (1956), 100-107.

Duncombe, David C. "The Evaluation of University Covenant Communities: A Critique and a Proposal." Report prepared for the Danforth Study of Campus Ministries, 1965, and published in extract as "An Experiment in Evaluation of Faith and Life Communities" in *The Church, the University and Social Policy.* Ed. Kenneth Underwood. Middletown, Conn.: Wesleyan University Press, 1969, III.

———. "Some Empirically Verifiable Correlates of the Christian Life as Derived from Protestant Thought." Unpublished doctoral dissertation, Yale University, 1966.

Dymond, Rosalind F. "Interpersonal Perception and Marital Happiness," *Canadian Journal of Psychology,* VIII (1954), 164-71.

———. "Personality and Empathy," *JCP,* XIV (1950), 343-50.

D'Zurilla, Thomas J. "Recall Efficiency and Mediating Cognitive Events in 'Experimental Repression.'" *Journal of Personality and Social Psychology,* I (1965), 253-57.

Eriksen, Charles W. "Defense Against Ego-Threat in Memory and Perception." *JASP,* XLVII (1952), 230-35.

Festinger, Leon *A Theory of Cognitive Dissonance.* Evanston, Ill.: Row, Peterson & Co., 1957.

Fisher, Seymour, and Fisher, Rhoda L. "The Effects of Personal Insecurity on Reactions to Unfamiliar Music," *Journal of Social Psychology,* XXXIV (1951), 265-73.

Frenkel-Brunswik, Else. "Intolerance of Ambiguity as an Emotional and Perceptual Personality Variable," *JP,* XVIII (1949-50), 108-43.

Freud, Sigmund. *A General Introduction to Psychoanalysis.* New York: Washington Square Press, 1960.

Gardner, Riley W., *et al.* "Cognitive Control: A Study of Individual Consistency in Cognitive Behavior," *Psychological Issues,* I (1959), 1-185.

Gergen, Kenneth J. "The Effects of Interaction Goals and Personalistic Feedback on the Presentation of the Self," *Journal of Personality and Social Psychology,* I (1965), 413-24.

Goslin, David A. "Accuracy of Self-Perception and Social Acceptance," *Sociometry,* XXV (1962), 283-96.

Grossman, David. "The Construction and Validation of Two Insight Inventories," *JCP,* XV (1951), 109-14.

Harvey, O. J. "Personality Factors in Resolution of Conceptual Incongruities," *Sociometry,* XXV (1962), 336-52.

Holt, Robert R. "The Accuracy of Self-evaluation: Its Measurement and Some of Its Personological Correlates," *JCP,* XV (1951), 95-101.

Holzman, Wayne H. "Personality Structure," *Annual Review of Psychology,* XVI (1965), 119-56.

Kaplan, Joy M. "Predicting Memory Behavior from Cognitive Attitudes Toward Instability," *American Psychologist,* VII (1952), 322.

Kenny, Douglas T., and Ginsberg, Rose. "The Specificity of Intolerance of Ambiguity Measures," *JASP,* LVI (1958), 300-305.

Klein, George S., and Schlesinger, Herbert J. "Perceptual Attitudes Toward Instability: I. Prediction of Apparent Movement Experiences from Rorschach Responses," *JP,* XIX (1951), 289-302.

Lazarus, Richard S., and Longo, Nicholas. "The Consistency of Psychological Defenses Against Threat," *JASP* XLVIII (1953), 495-99.

Levine, Jacob, and Abelson, Robert. "Humor as a Disturbing Stimulus," *Journal of General Psychology,* LX (1959), 191-200.

Levinger, George, and Clark, James. "Emotional Factors in the Forgetting of Word Associations," *JASP,* LXI (1962), 99-105.

Lowenfield, John. "Negative Affect as a Causal Factor in the Occurrence of Repression, Subsception, and Perceptual Defense," *JP,* XXIX (1961), 54-63.

Luchins, Abraham S. "The Einstellung Test of Rigidity: Its Relation to Concreteness of Thinking," *JCP,* XV (1951), 303-10.

Luft, Joseph. "Implicit Hypotheses and Clinical Predictions," *JASP,* XLV (1950), 156-60.

McDavid, John. "Personality and Situational Determinants of Conformity," *JASP,* LVIII (1959), 241-46.

———. "Personality Correlates with Two Kinds of Conforming Behavior," *JP,* XXXII (1964), 420-35.

Martin, Barclay. "Intolerance of Ambiguity in Interpersonal and Perceptual Behavior," *JP,* XXII (1954), 494-503.

Mathews, Anne, and Wertheimer, Michael. "A 'Pure' Measure of Perceptual Defense Uncontaminated by Response Supression," *JASP,* LVII (1958), 373-76.

Millon, Theodore. "Authoritarianism, Intolerance of Ambiguity, and Rigidity Under Ego- and Task-involving Conditions," *JASP*, LV (1957), 29-33.

Murstein, Bernard I. *Theory and Research in Projective Techniques (Emphasizing the TAT)*. New York: Wiley, 1963.

Nelson, Sherman E. "Psychosexual Conflicts and Defenses in Visual Perception," *JASP*, LI (1955), 427-33.

Perloe, Sidney I. "Inhibition as a Determinant of Perceptual Defense," *Perceptual and Motor Skills*, XI (1960), 59-66.

Roberts, Alan H., and Jessor, Richard. "Authoritarianism, Punitiveness, and Perceived Social Status," *JASP*, LVI (1958), 311-14.

Rokeach, Milton. "Attitude as a Determinant of Distortions in Recall," *JASP*, XLVII (1952), 482-88.

Sanford, Nevitt, and Risser, Joseph. "What Are the Conditions of Self-defensive Forgetting?" *JP*, XVII (1949), 244-60.

Sheehan, Neil. "Two Sides of Our Side," *New York Times Book Review*, May 14, 1967, p. 3.

Siegal, Sidney. "Certain Determinants and Correlates of Authoritarianism," *Genetic Psychology Monographs*, XLIX (1954), 187-229.

Taft, Ronald. "Intolerance of Ambiguity and Ethnocentrism," *JCP*, XX (1956), 153-54.

Temerlin, Maurice K. "One Determinant of the Capacity to Free-associate in Psychotherapy," *JASP*, LIII (1956), 16-18.

Tolor, Alexander, and Reznikoff, Marvin. "A New Approach to Insight: a Preliminary Report," *Journal of Nervous and Mental Disease*, CXXX (1960), 286-96.

Traux, Charles B. "The Repression Response to Implied Failure as a Function of the Hysteria-Psychasthenia Index," *JASP*, LV (1957), 188-93.

Wesley, Elizabeth L. "Perseverative Behavior in a Concept Formation Task as a Function of Manifest Anxiety and Rigidity," *JASP*, XLVIII (1953), 129-34.

Wrench, David, and Endicott, Kirk. "Denial of Affect and Conformity." *Journal of Personality and Social Psychology*, I (1965), 484-86.

Zeller, Anchard F. "An Experimental Analogue of Repression: II. The Effect of Individual Failure and Success on Memory Measured by Learning," *Journal of Experimental Psychology*, XL (1950), 411-22.

INDEX

Abelson, Robert P., 102, 183
Abilities, 22
Abraham, 35, 36
Absoluteness, 43
Accurate perception, 112-16
Acquiescence, 58
Acquired skills, abilities, and characteristics, 63
Affection, 92-93
Ahab, 120
Ainsworth, Leonard H., 46, 161-62
Aloofness, 41
Altruism, 142
Ambiguity, 44, 46-48, 53, 187
  being aware of, 66
  toleration of, 43, 51
Amnesia for failures, 69
Anger, 65, 92
Anti-type, 54
Anxiety, 38, 52, 154
Apprehension, 38, 66
Aptitude, peculiar, 184, 186
Argument, negative, 21
Asceticism, 142
Assurances, seeking after, 36
Authoritarian personality, 160
Authority, 34
Awareness, degree of, 73

Barth, Karl, 172
Behavior, 20, 62
  inappropriate, 144
  moralistic, 166
  reasonable and responsive, 151
Behavioral expectations, 179, 181
Belenky, Robert L., 133

Belief, 125
  and behavior, 165
  as a refuge, 124
  sign of, 17
Believing, 15-17, 99-100
Bench marks, 19, 26, 147, 173
Bizarre experiences, 52
Blasphemy, appropriateness of, 93
Blind acceptance, 100
Bondage to alien self, 154
Bossom, Joseph, 48-49
Brehm, Jack W., 165
Bronfenbrenner, Urie, 134

Caleb, 118-19
Calvin, John, 30, 86, 114, 143, 175
Cartoons, 102
Casuistry, risk of new, 182
Cautiousness, 154
Certainty, distrust of, 37
Certitude, creation of, 43
Characteristics of mature Christian life, 20, 22, 45
Christ
  all things pure in, 88
  at work, 20, 88
  body of, 85, 115, 175-76
  humanity of, 88
  power of, 85
  redemptive work of, 146
  responding to, 146
  revelation of, 113
  spirit of, 142
Christian
  behavior, 20
  belief and confession, 30
  community, 115

199

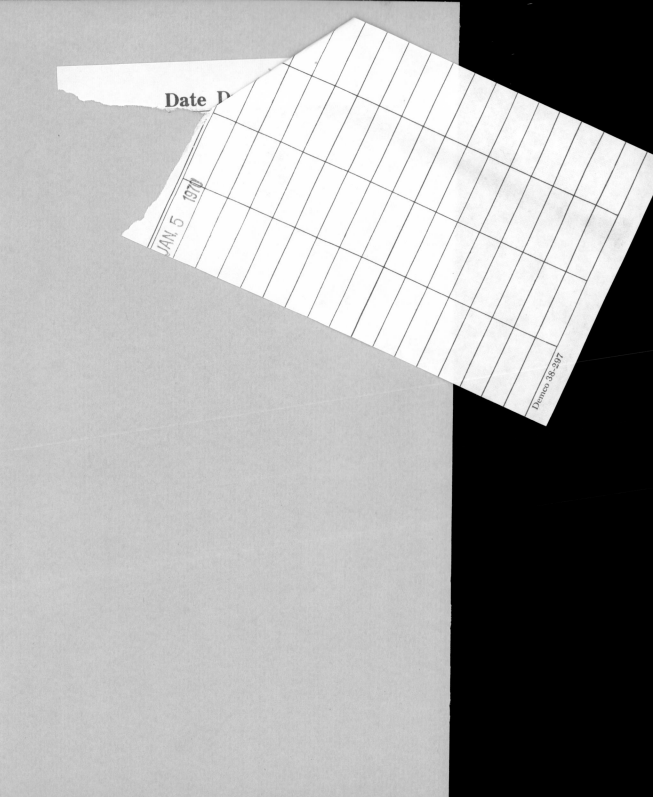